PBS LiteracyLink®
Workplace Essential Skills

COMMUNICATION & WRITING

by Karen Harrington

LiteracyLink is a joint project of the PBS, Kentucky Educational Television, the National Center on Adult Literacy, and the Kentucky Department of Education. This project is funded in whole, or in part, by the Star Schools Program of the USDE under contract #R203D60001.

Acknowledgments

LiteracyLink® Advisory Board

Dr. Drew Albritton, American Association for Adult and Continuing Education

Peggy Barber, American Library Association

Anthony Buttino, WNED-TV

Dr. Anthony Carnevale, Educational Testing Service

Dr. Patricia Edwards, Michigan State University

Maggi Gaines, Baltimore Reads, Inc.

Dr. Milton Goldberg, National Alliance for Business

Columbus Hartwell, Exodus

Jan Hawkins, Center for Children and Technology, Education Development Corporation, Inc.

Neal Johnson, Educational Testing Service

Dr. Cynthia Johnston, Central Piedmont Community College

Thomas Kinney, American Association of Adult and Continuing Education

Dr. Jacqueline E. Korengel, Kentucky Department for Adult Ed and Literacy

Michael O'Brian, Certain Teed Corporation

Rafael Ramirez, U.S. Deptartment of Education

Dr. Emma Rhodes, Formerly of Arkansas Department of Education

Dr. Ahmed Sabie, Kentucky Department of Adult Education and Literacy

Tony Sarmiento, Worker Centered Learning, Working for America Institute

Dr. Steve Steurer, Correctional Education Association

Dr. Alice Tracy, Correctional Education Association

Dr. Fran Tracy-Mumford, Delaware Department of Adult/Community Education

Dr. Terilyn Turner, Community Education, St. Paul Public Schools

Dr. Renee Westcott, Central Piedmont Community College

Ex Officio Advisory Members

Joan Aucher, GED Testing Service

Cheryl Garnette, U.S. Department of Education

Dr. Andrew Hartman, National Institute for Literacy

Dr. Mary Lovell, U.S. Department of Education

Ronald Pugsley, U.S. Department of Education

Dr. Linda Roberts, U.S. Department of Education

Joe Wilkes, U.S. Department of Education

LiteracyLink Partners

LiteracyLink is a joint project of the Public Broadcasting Service, Kentucky Educational Television, the National Center on Adult Literacy, and the Kentucky Department of Education. This project is funded in whole, or in part, by the Star Schools Program of the USDE under contract #R203D60001.

Special thanks to the Kentucky Department for Adult Education and Literacy, Workforce Development Cabinet for its help on this project and for its vision and commitment to excellence in helping provide superior adult education products and services.

Workbook Production

Developer:
Learning Unlimited, Oak Park, Illinois

Design:
PiperStudios Inc., Chicago, Illinois

Cover Design and Layout:
By Design, Lexington, Kentucky

Project Consultant:
Milli Fazey, KET, Lexington, Kentucky

Production Manager:
Margaret Norman, KET, Lexington, Kentucky

• •

ISBN 1-881020-35-5
ISBN 978-1-881020-35-6

Table of Contents

To the Teacher

The purpose of the *Workplace Essential Skills* series is to enable adult learners to become better informed and more highly skilled for the changing world of work. The materials are aimed at adults who are at the pre-GED (6th- to 8th-grade) reading level.

Twenty-four *Workplace Essential Skills* **television programs** model the application of basic skills within the context of pre-employment and workplace settings. The four accompanying **workbooks** present instruction, practice, and application of the critical skills that are represented in the programs:

- *Employment*
- *Communication & Writing*
- *Reading*
- *Mathematics*

The series includes a utilization program for instructors and an overview program for learners.

The series also includes a **teacher's guide** for instructors and an **assessment instrument** to help learners and instructors determine the most effective course of study in the *Workplace Essential Skills* series.

Each lesson in the *Communication & Writing* workbook corresponds to one of the seven employability television programs in the *Workplace Essential Skills* series. The topics in the *Communication & Writing* workbook and the video programs are based on common labor market and workplace tasks.

Basic skills, problem solving, and decision making are integrated into every lesson. Additionally, interdisciplinary connections are inserted throughout the books for practice in real-world reading, writing, communication, math, and technology skills.

Taken together, the features and components of the *Workplace Essential Skills* instructional program provide a comprehensive grounding in the knowledge and skills learners need to succeed in the world of work. By also utilizing the ***LiteracyLink*** on-line component (see page vii), learners will begin to develop some of the computer literacy and Internet know-how needed to advance in the workplace of today and tomorrow.

Many of the skills covered in *Workplace Essential Skills* also provide a foundation for GED-level work in the areas of reading, math, and writing. Because high school completion is an important prerequisite for advancement in the work world, learners should be encouraged to go on to GED-level study when they are ready to do so. The ***LiteracyLink*** GED videos, print, and on-line materials (available in the year 2000) will provide an ideal context for learners to prepare for the GED tests and fulfill the requirement of high school equivalency.

To the Learner

Welcome to *Workplace Essential Skills: Communication & Writing*. This workbook has been designed to help you learn more about the ideas and skills presented in Programs 9–15 of the *Workplace Essential Skills* series. Take time to read about some of the features in this book.

1. The **Skills Preview** on pages 1–8 will help you discover which video programs and workbook lessons are most important for you. You can use the **Skills Preview Evaluation Chart** on page 10 to make your own personal study plan.

2. Each workbook lesson goes with a program in the television series. The lessons in this workbook cover Programs 9–15. Use the program number and title to find the corresponding tape and workbook lesson. After the opening page and **Objectives**, each lesson is divided into two parts:

   Before You Watch starts you thinking about the topics in the video program.

   - **Sneak Preview:** Exercise to preview some of the key concepts from the program.
   - **Answers for Sneak Preview:** Answers to the preview exercise.
   - **Feedback:** Information to help you personalize your work.
   - **Vocabulary:** Key terms from the lesson and their definitions.

   After You Watch allows you to apply skills that you saw in the program.

   - **Key Points from the Video Program:** List that summarizes the program.
   - **Situations:** Real-world problem solving from the health care, manufacturing, service, retail, and construction industries.
   - **Information:** In-depth information about important workplace concepts.
   - **WorkTips:** Hints for success in the world of work.
   - **WorkSkills:** Exercise that enables you to apply what you have learned.
   - **Connections:** Extension of workplace skills through practice in other content areas. (*Write It, Tech Tip, Read It, Math Matters,* and *Communicate*)
   - **Review:** Section that lets you put all of your new workplace knowledge together.

3. The **Skills Review** allows you to evaluate what you have learned.

4. The **Answer Key** starts on page 161. There you can find answers to the exercises in each lesson, often with explanations, as well as samples of filled-in forms and documents.

5. The **Glossary,** which starts on page 181, includes key terms and definitions.

6. You can use the alphabetized **Index,** which starts on page 183, to look up information about employment issues.

7. A **Reference Handbook,** found on pages 187–196, is a helpful resource for you to access at any time. References to the handbook are listed throughout the book.

The LiteracyLink® System

Welcome to the *LiteracyLink* system. This workbook is one part of an educational system for adult learners and adult educators.

LiteracyLink consists of these learning tools:

Television programs
broadcast on
public television
and in adult
learning centers

Computer-based materials
available
through a
connection to the Internet

Workbooks
print-based
instruction
and practice

If you are working with *LiteracyLink* materials, you have a clear educational advantage. As you develop your knowledge and skills, you are also working with video and computer technology. This is the technology required to succeed in today's workplace, training programs, and colleges.

Content of the *LiteracyLink* System

The *LiteracyLink* system allows you to choose what you need to meet your goals. It consists of instruction and practice in the areas of:

Workplace Essential Skills
- Employment
  Pre-Employment and On-the-Job Skills
- Communication & Writing
  Listening, Speaking, and Writing Skills
- Reading
  Charts, Forms, Documents, and Manuals
- Mathematics
  Whole Numbers, Decimals, Fractions, and Percents

GED Preparation Series
- Language Arts Reading
  Fiction, Nonfiction, Poetry, Drama and Informational
- Language Arts Writing
  Essay Writing, Sentence Structure, Grammar, and Mechanics
- Social Studies
  U.S. History, World History, Geography, Civics and Government, and Economics
- Science
  Life Sciences, Earth and Space Sciences, Chemistry, and Physics
- Mathematics
  Arithmetic, Data Analysis, Algebra, and Geometry

Instructional Units

Units of study are used to organize *LiteracyLink's* instruction. For example, the first unit in this book is The Language of Work. To study this topic, you can use a video, workbook lesson, and computer. You will be able to easily find what you need since each workbook unit has the same title as a video and related Internet activities.

Getting Started With the System

It is possible to use each *LiteracyLink* component separately. However, you will make the best use of *LiteracyLink* if you use all of the parts. You can make this work in a way that is best for you through the *LiteracyLink* Internet site.

On the Internet site, you will take a Welcome Tour and establish your Home Space. The Home Space is your starting point for working through the online portion of *LiteracyLink*. It is also a place where you can save all of your online work.

An important part of the online system is LitHelper℠. This helps you to identify your strengths and weaknesses. LitHelper℠ helps you to develop an individualized study plan. The online LitLearner® materials, together with the videos and workbooks, provide hundreds of learning opportunities. Go to http://www.pbs.org/literacy to access the online material.

For Teachers

Parts of *LiteracyLink* have been developed for adult educators and service providers. LitTeacher® is an online professional development system. It provides a number of resources including PeerLit℠ a database of evaluated websites. At http://www.pbs.org/literacy you can also access *LitTeacher*.

Who's Responsible for *LiteracyLink*?

LiteracyLink was sparked by a five-year grant by the U.S. Department of Education. The following partners have contributed to the development of the *LiteracyLink* system:
- PBS Adult Learning Service
- Kentucky Educational Television (KET)
- The National Center on Adult Literacy (NCAL) of the University of Pennsylvania
- The Kentucky Department of Education

The *LiteracyLink* partners wish you the very best in achieving your educational goals.

Skills Preview

Questions 1–8 are based on the following situation.

SALE SALE

RETAIL: Renaldo is an electronics salesclerk at Merchandise City. He sees a customer reading the description on the box of a telephone answering machine.

Renaldo [*smiling*]: Hi! What kind of answering machine do you want?

Customer: I don't know. I'm looking for a machine that will save me from having to listen to the messages my teenagers get. Their friends leave hundreds of them. You know how teenagers are!

Renaldo: It sounds like you want a machine with voice mailboxes.

Customer [*wrinkling his brow*]: Yeah, I guess so...

Renaldo [*speaking energetically*]: A machine with voice mailboxes routes the calls for one to four people. When callers want to leave messages, they specify which mailbox they want the message routed to. Then the listener only listens to the messages in his or her mailbox. Do you think the mailboxes would help you out?

Customer [*nodding*]: I think so. I could set up three mailboxes—one for me and one for each of my two kids. Then I would just listen to the messages in my mailbox. Right?

Renaldo: That's right! Let me show you what we have.

Write *True* if the statement is true; *False* if it is false.

_____ 1. By smiling pleasantly, Renaldo tried to make a positive impression.

_____ 2. Renaldo should have talked about his children when the customer said, "You know how teenagers are!"

_____ 3. Renaldo did not listen carefully when the customer described his needs.

_____ 4. The customer's wrinkled brow was a nonverbal message that he didn't understand what Renaldo had said.

_____ 5. When Renaldo asked, "Do you think the mailboxes would help you out?" he was checking whether the customer understood his explanation.

_____ 6. The customer checked his understanding by restating what he had heard.

_____ 7. Renaldo spoke in a negative tone of voice.

_____ 8. Renaldo communicated well with the customer.

Questions 9–11 are based on the following situation.

SERVICE: Frank, the owner of a pizzeria, has heard from one of the pizza delivery drivers that Parul, another driver, keeps parking his car illegally or blocking the alley behind the restaurant.

Frank: Parul, I've told you before not to park illegally or block the alley with your car. I've got enough problems without worrying about the neighbors complaining because you can't follow the rules.

Parul: Don't they have anything better to do? I'm just trying to do my job!

Frank: I know. But our goal is to sell and deliver pizzas, not to annoy the neighbors. Why don't you park somewhere else, like the other drivers?

Parul: Because the spaces are farther away. I'll lose time and not get as many orders.

Frank: Parul, how would you feel if one of the other drivers got more orders than you because he cheated and didn't follow the rules?

Parul: I guess I'd feel it wasn't fair. I'd be pretty mad about it.

Frank: Right! How about if you follow the rules and try to get along with everyone?

Parul: OK, Frank. It won't happen again.

Choose the best answer to each question.

9. Frank gave feedback to Parul to

    (1) show Parul who's boss
    (2) punish Parul for cheating
    (3) uncover and solve a problem
    (4) make Parul feel guilty

10. Frank kept the communication on task in the beginning by

    (1) reminding Parul that he's talked to him about this before
    (2) ignoring Parul's comment about the neighbors
    (3) asking Parul how he'd feel if a driver cheated him
    (4) telling Parul to follow the rules

11. What cause of the problem did Frank discover?

    (1) Parul didn't like the neighbors.
    (2) Parul parked illegally and blocked the alley.
    (3) Parul just wanted to do his job.
    (4) Parul parked nearby so he could get more orders.

Questions 12–18 are based on the following situation.

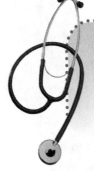

HEALTH CARE: Over the past month, six patients of United Community Hospital's emergency department (ED) have fallen and been injured. The head of the risk management department has called together a team of employees to solve this problem.

Manager: Our accident reports show that the number of patient falls in ED has increased during the past 30 days. How can we improve safety?

ED Nurse: Well, one problem is that since the ED staff has been reduced, security guards have sometimes had to help lift patients into beds and wheelchairs, and some of them don't do it right.

Security Guard: That is a problem, but it's not the guards' fault, really. The real problem is not the use of guards but the use of *untrained* guards. Some of the newer security people haven't been trained in patient transport procedures.

Human Resources Representative: Sounds as if we need to have a few sessions with all guards to demonstrate proper procedure.

Maintenance Worker: I'll tell you something else. Spills and other hazards aren't reported quickly. Monday, after that big snowstorm, the ED entrance was slippery but nobody reported it. We check the entrance hourly, but in bad weather, ED should alert us if problems arise.

ED Admission Clerk: We're awfully busy, but I guess we could make a point of checking more often. If the ED staff lets us know about spills, we can call maintenance immediately for them.

Manager: Good idea. In fact, we've had two good ideas. Let's hear more.

Write *True* if the statement is true; *False* if it is false.

_____ 12. The team contains employees with different jobs and therefore with a wide range of experiences.

_____ 13. The team's goal is to share stories about the problem.

_____ 14. Each member of the team should share responsibility for developing improved safety procedures.

_____ 15. Each team member shows leadership qualities.

_____ 16. The team is likely to fail because the members don't work well together.

_____ 17. The employees are using teamwork to solve a problem.

_____ 18. The manager shows respect for the team members by letting them participate in decisions.

Questions 19–21 are based on the following situation.

SERVICE: Lin is a customer satisfaction representative for Country's Goods sportswear, a chain of stores that also markets clothing through catalog sales. Lin is speaking to a customer on the telephone.

Customer: When I phoned in the catalog order from your store, the phone rep told me that the only difference between the large sweater in the regular and tall sizes was length. But when I got the sweater, I knew it was bigger all the way around. I can't believe he lied to me like that!

Lin: Let's see if we can correct this. Do you want a different size?

Customer: I need a medium sweater in the tall size... but only if I'll still get the 10% discount that I got with my first order.

Lin: I can still give you the discount price.

Customer: OK. Another problem is that the sweater is a gift, and I need it tomorrow night.

Lin: If I send it by overnight mail, you'll have it tomorrow. And since there was a problem, I won't charge for delivery. Will that help?

Customer: Yes, it will. I like the way you resolved this problem.

Lin: It's our way of letting you know that we appreciate your business.

Choose the best answer to each question.

19. The way Lin handled the problem customer shows that she

    (1) understands the importance of customer satisfaction

    (2) feels the phone rep who caused the problem should solve it

    (3) wants to get the customer off the phone as soon as possible

    (4) is annoyed by the customer's unpleasant tone and demands

20. To provide for the customer's needs, Lin

    (1) apologized and promised to talk to the other phone rep

    (2) offered a solution and asked the customer if it was satisfactory

    (3) explained why the problem occurred and what to do about it

    (4) showed that the sizing is correct and the customer is wrong

21. Which of the following best describes Lin's approach?

    (1) Find out who is to blame and tell the supervisor.

    (2) Tell customers whatever you think will make them happy.

    (3) Don't take responsibility for other people's mistakes.

    (4) Focus on solutions and don't take criticism personally.

Questions 22–28 are based on the following message.

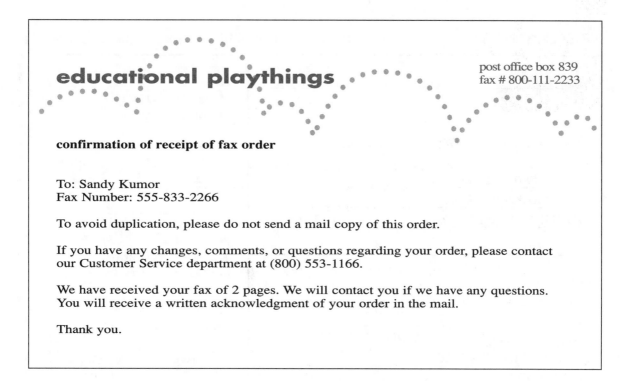

educational playthings

post office box 839
fax # 800-111-2233

confirmation of receipt of fax order

To: Sandy Kumor
Fax Number: 555-833-2266

To avoid duplication, please do not send a mail copy of this order.

If you have any changes, comments, or questions regarding your order, please contact our Customer Service department at (800) 553-1166.

We have received your fax of 2 pages. We will contact you if we have any questions. You will receive a written acknowledgment of your order in the mail.

Thank you.

Write *True* if the statement is true; *False* if it is false.

_____ 22. The message is a personal note.

_____ 23. The message is formatted as a fax memo.

_____ 24. The message is written in informal language.

_____ 25. The purpose of the message is to confirm a fax order and give instructions to the reader.

_____ 26. The message is well organized.

_____ 27. The writing is straightforward, courteous, and clear.

_____ 28. The message focuses on the needs of the reader.

Questions 29–33 are based on the following written communication.

POST EXPRESS AIRBILL Tracking Number 9949716 Sender's Copy

Date: _1/8/99_ Sender's Post Express Acct. #: _K119705_

From:
Sender's Name: _MICHAEL SOKOL_
Phone_____
Company _SOKOL & SONS, INC._
Address _250 MAIN STREET_
City _CITRUS GROVE_ State _FL_ ZIP _32900_

To:
Recipient's Name: _LAUREN McVICKERS_
Phone_____
Company _MANUFACTURING RESOURCES COMPANY_
Address _6043 W. 159th STREET_
City _ORLANDO_ State _FL_ ZIP _32010_

Service
☑ Overnight ☐ 2nd Day
☐ Saturday ☐ Freight

Packaging
☑ Letter ☐ Box ☐ Tube
_____
_____
_____

Payment/Bill to:
☑ Sender ☐ Recipient
☐ 3rd Party ☐ Credit Card

Post Express Acct. #_____
Credit Card #_____

Total Packages Total Charges
_1_ _$11.00_

Fill in each blank with the correct answer.

29. What is the purpose of the message?

_____

30. What format is the message in: form, letter, memo, or report?

_____

31. How does this format help the writer organize information?

_____

32. How does this format help the reader find information?

_____

33. What information is missing from the message?

_____

Questions 34–39 are based on the following letter.

COMMERCIAL DEVELOPERS

March 21, 1999

Hines Heater Company
581 Hyde Park Avenue
Hillside, Illinois 60162

Dear Sir or Madam:

On June 21, 1998, your distributor, Stevens Stoker & Heating Company, installed a new Hines #211A 2OS—3,990,000 Btu/hour complete gas steam section boiler at the Commercial Boulevard address listed below.

During this past winter the bolier shut off whenever the outside temperature dropped below zero degrees for two or more consecutive days. Stevens Stoker & Heating made numerous attempts to correct the problem, with the most recent work being done on February 12, 1999.

According to the manufacturer's warranty, the Hines Heater Company warrants the boiler for one year from the date of purchase, which means our warranty will expire on or about June 21 of this year. Since it is unlikely that the outside temperature will fall below zero degrees again this winter, we will not know whether the recent work by Stevens Stoker & Heating has corrected the problem in the boiler. Therefore, I am requesting an extension of the warranty until such time next winter that the outside temperature drops below zero degrees for two or more consecutive days.

Please respond in writing within 30 days after receiving this letter.

Very truly yours,

Ty Chooli

Ty Chooli
President

3098 W. Commercial Boulevard ▪ Twinsburg, Ohio 44087

Choose the best answer to each question.

34. What is the purpose of the letter?

    (1) to inform
    (2) to explain
    (3) to persuade
    (4) all of the above

35. Where is the specific purpose of the letter stated?

    (1) paragraph 1
    (2) paragraph 2
    (3) paragraph 3
    (4) paragraph 4

36. Which questions do the facts in the first paragraph answer? Circle all that apply.

    a. *When?*
    b. *What?*
    c. *Where?*

37. Who is the recipient of this letter?

    (1) Chooli Commercial Developers
    (2) Hines Heater Company
    (3) Stevens Stoker & Heating Company
    (4) Ty Chooli

38. Which of the following corrections should be made in paragraph 2?

    (1) Change *bolier* to *boiler.*
    (2) Correct the first sentence so it's not a fragment.
    (3) Remove the capital letters from *Stoker* and *Heating.*
    (4) Remove the comma from *February 12, 1999.*

39. What should the writer do after making the correction to paragraph 2? Why?

    _____

Skills Preview Answer Key

1. True
2. False
3. False
4. True
5. True
6. True
7. False
8. True
9. (3) uncover and solve a problem
10. (2) ignoring Parul's comment about the neighbors
11. (4) Parul parked nearby so he could get more orders.
12. True
13. False
14. True
15. True
16. False
17. True
18. True
19. (1) understands the importance of customer satisfaction
20. (2) offered a solution and asked the customer if it was satisfactory
21. (4) Focus on solutions and don't take criticism personally.
22. False
23. True
24. False
25. True
26. False
27. True
28. True
29. to give mailing instructions
30. form
31. It tells what facts to include and where to write them.
32. All information is clearly labeled.
33. phone numbers
34. (4) all of the above
35. (3) paragraph 3
36. a, b, c
37. (2) Hines Heater Company
38. (1) Change *bolier* to *boiler.*
39. proofread to make sure the letter is error-free

Skills Preview Evaluation Chart

Circle the question numbers that you answered correctly. Then fill in the number of questions you got correct for each program lesson. Find the total number correct, and focus your work on the lessons you had trouble with.

Program Lesson	Question Number	Number Correct/Total
9: *The Language of Work* Speaking and Listening, Identifying Nonverbal Communication, Developing Effective Communication Skills	1, 2, 3, 4, 5, 6, 7, 8	____/8
10: *Communicating with Co-Workers and Supervisors* Communicating Successfully with Co-Workers, Communicating with Supervisors, Resolving Conflicts with Co-Workers and Supervisors	9, 10, 11	____/3
11: *Working Together* Developing Teamwork Skills, Participating on a Work Team, Being Part of an Effective Team	12, 13, 14, 15, 16, 17, 18	____/7
12: *Communicating with Customers* Understanding the Importance of Customer Satisfaction, Providing for Customers' Needs, Working with Difficult Customers	19, 20, 21	____/3
13: *A Process for Writing* Becoming an Effective Writer, Understanding Workplace Writing, Using Appropriate Language	22, 23, 24, 25, 26, 27, 28	____/7
14: *Supplying Information: Directions, Forms, and Charts* Writing Down Information, Working with Forms, Using Charts Effectively	29, 30, 31, 32, 33	____/5
15: *Writing Memos and Letters* Planning Written Communication, Organizing and Writing First Drafts, Writing and Distributing Final Drafts	34, 35, 36, 37, 38, 39	____/6
	Total	____/39

WHAT YOUR SCORE MEANS

If you got 36–39 correct: You have an excellent understanding of workplace communication.

If you got 32–35 correct: You have a good understanding of workplace communication. See which topic areas the questions you missed belong to, and focus on these topics.

If you got 28–31 correct: You need to develop your communication skills in the workplace. See which topic areas the questions you missed belong to, and focus on these topics.

If you got less than 28 correct: You need to watch the videos and work through the lessons in the workbook to learn about communication skills in the workplace.

BEFORE you WATCH

The Language of Work

The video program you are about to watch shows problems that can occur at work when people don't communicate well. You will see how good **communication** skills help employees and companies.

As you watch the video, look for times when people misunderstand each other. Notice why the misunderstandings occurred: Did the people express themselves clearly? Did they listen to each other?

Most people spend a large part of their day communicating. Do you speak to others in person or on the phone? Listen to and observe others? Write or read information? These are forms of communication. In fact, even the sound of your voice, your smiles, and other **body language** send messages. Do people understand your messages as you intend them to? Do you understand the messages others send to you? At work and at home, you need to communicate!

Sneak Preview

This exercise previews some of the concepts from Program 9. After you answer the questions, use the Feedback on page 13 to help set your learning goals.

RETAIL: You are a salesclerk in a shoe store. A customer picks up a navy-blue shoe but frowns as she looks at it. You walk up.

"Hi," you say with a smile. "How can I help you?"

"Well," she says, "this shoe is the color I want, but the heel is too high. And the price is way too much!"

You ask, "Would you prefer an inch-and-a-half heel? It's more comfortable but still dressy enough for work and evening wear."

"Yeah, I guess so," she replies. "But these prices . . ."

You hand her a shoe in black and say, "Is this closer to what you're looking for? It has the lower heel. Plus it's on sale!"

The customer replies, "That's more like it."

You say, "I'll go look for the shoe. What size do you need?"

The customer sits down, glances at her watch, and snaps, "8B."

Figuring she's in a hurry, you say, "I'll be right back." You soon return with red shoes. Noticing her puzzled look, you say, "I'm sorry, all we have in your size is red. But if they fit, I'll have a navy pair sent to you. I called, and our other store has them."

The customer tries on the shoes. "These do fit." she says. Then she wrinkles her forehead and says, "I'm not paying for shipping!"

"You won't have to," you calmly reply. "It's our store policy to get you the shoes you want at no extra charge to you."

"Well," she smiles, "in that case, you've made a sale!"

You ask the customer for her driver's license and credit card, then fill out the charge slip. She signs it. After you check her signature, you return her license and credit card, and say, "I'll have the shoes sent right away. If you have any problems, just give me a call. Here's my card."

The customer looks pleased. "I appreciate your help," she replies.

Answer these questions based on the situation.

1. List four forms of communication you and the customer used.

    _____   _____

    _____   _____

2. Briefly describe two times when misunderstandings could have occurred.

_____

_____

Match the letter of each communication skill with the situation that illustrates it.

Details

_____ 3. You correctly "read" the customer's messages when she frowns, looks at her watch, and raises her eyebrows.

_____ 4. When your store doesn't have the right shoes, you call the other store to locate the pair the customer wants.

_____ 5. You apologize for not having the correct color in stock and explain store policy.

_____ 6. You speak calmly when you tell the customer shipping is free.

_____ 7. You listen carefully to the customer and ask questions about what she wants.

Communication Skill

a. Be an active listener.

b. Explain ideas politely and clearly.

c. Be aware of body language.

d. Use a positive tone of voice.

e. Use problem-solving strategies.

Feedback for Sneak Preview

• If you got all of the answers right . . .   you have a basic understanding of the communication process. While watching the video, focus on how poor communication can cause problems in the workplace.

• If you missed question 1 or 2 . . .   you need to work on your basic communication skills.

• If you missed question 3 . . .   you need to work on your nonverbal communication skills.

• If you missed question 4 or 6 . . .   you need to work on developing effective communication skills.

• If you missed question 5 or 7 . . .   you need to work on your speaking and listening skills.

Vocabulary for *The Language of Work*

active listening strategies	steps for concentrating on and understanding messages
body language	gestures, looks, and postures that communicate messages
communication	the process of sending and receiving messages
customer service	the help a business offers its clients to make a good impression about its products or services
ethnic	relating to a large group of people classed according to common racial, national, religious, or cultural backgrounds or origins
miscommunications	misunderstandings caused by poor communications
nonverbal communication	sending and receiving messages through gestures, facial expressions, and voice qualities
orientation	the process of acquainting oneself with a business, product, or job
perceives	sees and interprets
prejudices	opinions formed without knowing a person or situation firsthand
salutation	a spoken or written greeting
service standards	written or spoken "rules" that explain customer service goals and the employee's role in meeting them
solicitation	the process of asking for something, such as information
swipe card	a card, similar to a credit card, that has a magnetic strip containing information about the user
touch screen	a computer screen on which a person communicates by touching various options

PBS LiteracyLink®

Now watch Program 9.

After you watch, work on:
- pages 15–30 in this workbook
- Internet activities at www.pbs.org/literacy

AFTER you WATCH

program **9**

The Language of Work

On the following pages, you will learn more about the ideas discussed in the video program and have an opportunity to develop your skills.

Think About the Key Points from the Video Program

When you are learning a new job or task, an employer expects you to:
- Listen carefully to instructions.
- Use effective speaking skills.

Once on the job, you need to:
- Use positive body language.
- Speak in a positive tone of voice, especially during disagreements.

When **miscommunications** occur, you need to:
- Find the cause of the misunderstanding.
- Find a common ground to understand the other person's point of view and solve the problem.

Speaking and Listening

As you saw in the video program, effective communication is key to the workplace. Most business takes place when people speak and listen to each other face to face or on the phone.

Communication is a give-and-take process. When speaking, you must word your messages clearly and completely. As the speaker, you also must look for signs that the listener doesn't understand—and be ready to state your message again more clearly. When listening, you must focus on the message—and ask questions if you don't understand.

How can you tell if communication is effective? See if the other person understood your message as you intended. Note how well you understood the message the person sent to you. If you're not sure, ask!

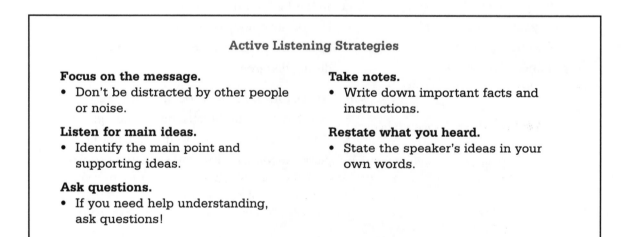

Think of a time you communicated with someone today. Fill in the chart below.

People Involved	Subject	Effectiveness of Communication (Explain.)

Using Active Listening Strategies

To truly understand what someone is saying, use **active listening strategies.** Concentrate and make sure you understand what you hear.

Active Listening Strategies

Focus on the message.
- Don't be distracted by other people or noise.

Listen for main ideas.
- Identify the main point and supporting ideas.

Ask questions.
- If you need help understanding, ask questions!

Take notes.
- Write down important facts and instructions.

Restate what you heard.
- State the speaker's ideas in your own words.

Evaluate your listening skills. Write *True* if the statement is True; *False* if it is False. Then think about ways to listen better.

_____ I feel uncomfortable asking for explanations.

_____ I often do something else while someone is talking to me.

_____ I stop listening when the message gets too complicated.

_____ If the way someone talks annoys me, I ignore the person.

Speaking Effectively

On the job, you may be responsible for passing on information or telling someone what to do. Work discussions are very different from personal conversations. Here are some practical guidelines.

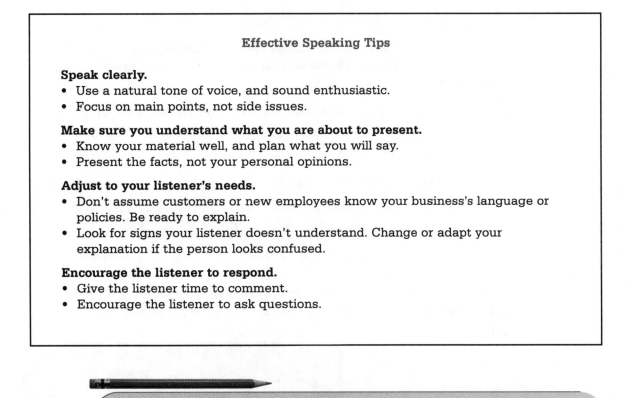

Effective Speaking Tips

Speak clearly.
- Use a natural tone of voice, and sound enthusiastic.
- Focus on main points, not side issues.

Make sure you understand what you are about to present.
- Know your material well, and plan what you will say.
- Present the facts, not your personal opinions.

Adjust to your listener's needs.
- Don't assume customers or new employees know your business's language or policies. Be ready to explain.
- Look for signs your listener doesn't understand. Change or adapt your explanation if the person looks confused.

Encourage the listener to respond.
- Give the listener time to comment.
- Encourage the listener to ask questions.

Think of someone who is an effective speaker. The person might be a politician, TV personality, or someone else in public life. Or it might be someone you know, such as a teacher or religious leader. On a separate piece of paper, write five reasons why this person is an effective speaker. Which techniques can *you* use?

SERVICE: Tony has a new job as a server. At other restaurants, he wrote the order on a ticket, handed it to the cook, added up the prices, and gave the ticket to the customer for payment. However, this new restaurant is different. Tony has to enter the order on the **touch screen** of a computerized ordering and payment system in the restaurant. Maria, Tony's boss, is explaining to Tony how to use the touch screen.

Communication Strategies

On this page and the next, you will see samples of the touch screens and Maria's explanations to Tony.

Imagine that you are in Tony's situation, learning new processes. Use the active listening strategies of *asking questions* and *restating* to write a comment or a question for Tony.

1. **Maria:** Tony, here is your personal **swipe card.** After you write the order on your ticket, bring the ticket over here. Then swipe the card along the top of the computer to access your tables.

    Tony: [*Sample question:*] *Which way should I hold the card when I swipe it?*

    _____

    _____

    _____

2. **Maria:** Here is your section, tables 13–20. Touch table 20 on the screen. Now touch a number for the number of guests at table 20. For 3 guests, touch the number 3.

    Tony:

    _____

    _____

    _____

    _____

    _____

    _____

3. **Maria:** On the left side of the screen you have a copy of a ticket. On the right side you have categories of food to order. Next you will touch a type of food. Press "Appetizers."

Tony:

_____

_____

_____

4. **Maria:** This is the next screen. The ticket is still on the left. Each of these buttons stands for one of our appetizers. Push number 1 for person 1 at the table.

Tony:

_____

_____

_____

_____

_____

_____

_____

_____

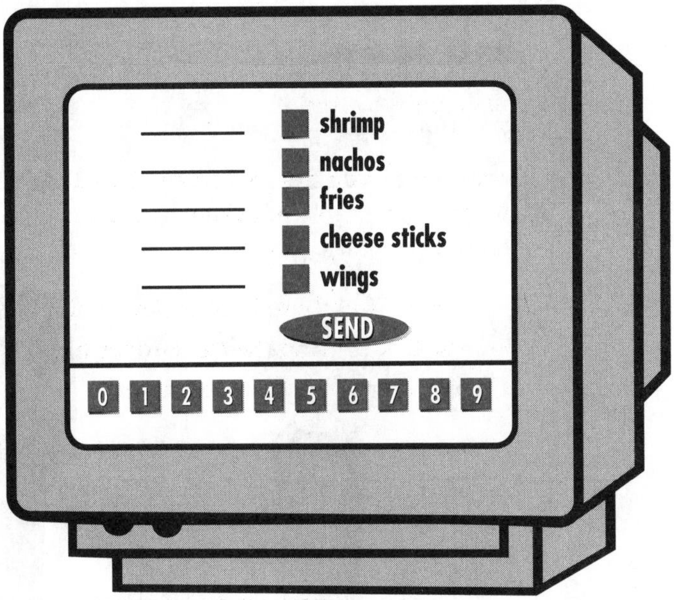

5. **Maria:** Now push the screen button for the nachos appetizer that person 1 ordered. When you have entered the appetizers for each person—and anything else they've ordered at this time—press the Send button at the bottom of the screen.

Tony:

_____

_____

_____

WRITE IT •

Reread Maria's directions to Tony, and look at the touch screen. On a separate piece of paper, write notes that Tony could refer to as he is beginning to work with the computer screen.

Identifying Nonverbal Communication

In the video program, you saw how people communicated nonverbally, or without words. They smiled, made eye contact, frowned, gestured, and maybe even stomped off. Each of those "nonverbal clues" sent a message about the person's feelings and attitudes. Sometimes, the **nonverbal communication** supported what the person was saying. Other times, the body language was different from the spoken message and sent a mixed, or confusing, message.

At work, be aware of your body language and the messages it may be sending. Make sure your nonverbal clues "match" what you say. Also be aware of the body language of co-workers and customers. Ask yourself what feelings their nonverbal clues convey. Employers look for employees who can "read" situations and solve problems before they get out of hand.

How is each person feeling?

1._____ 2._____ 3._____

Depending on the situation and the words being spoken, a person's body language may mean different things. When you interpret body language, think about the "big picture"—the situation in which it is used.

Communicating through Gestures

Employers need employees who look confident, enthusiastic, and interested in their job. Stand straight with your shoulders back and your head high. Smile, make eye contact, and use positive gestures and body language. You will feel more confident, and you will make a positive impression on others.

Check gestures that make a positive impression.

_____ 1. Drumming fingers on a table

_____ 2. Sitting up straight

_____ 3. Waving your arms as you speak

_____ 4. Stressing key points with your hands

_____ 5. Shaking hands firmly

_____ 6. Making eye contact

_____ 7. Sighing loudly

_____ 8. Smiling

_____ 9. Bowing your head

_____ 10. Pursing your lips

Using a Positive Tone of Voice

How you sound also affects how others perceive you. At work, speak calmly at a volume and speed that is comfortable for others. The chart below lists different voice qualities and their effects.

Voice Quality	Effect on Listener
High and squeaky	Irritating
Emotionless; monotonous	Boring
Whiny	Signals speaker is a complainer
Extremely low or soft	Difficult to hear
Very slow	Uninteresting
Very fast	Hard to understand
Unclear speech	Hard to understand
Loud and harsh	Causes fear and nervousness
Calm and smooth	Relaxing; calming
Expressive	Energetic; enthusiastic

Use the chart above to answer the following questions.

1. What qualities describe your voice? List them.

_____

2. Which qualities would you like to change? Why?

_____

_____

WorkSkills

SERVICE: Mai is in training for her new job as a clerk in the gift shop of the Majestic Hotel. It is part of a chain of hotels known for giving guests excellent service to ensure their comfort and satisfaction.

Part of Mai's **orientation,** or introduction to the job, includes learning about Majestic's basic **service standards,** which define her role in meeting the hotel's **customer service** goals. Mai has been given a card that describes Majestic Hotel's service goals and defines its service standards.

Communication Strategies

To understand your part in meeting a business's goals, you should carefully read information you are given about the business and your job.

Read the Majestic Hotel's service standards. Then answer the questions on page 23.

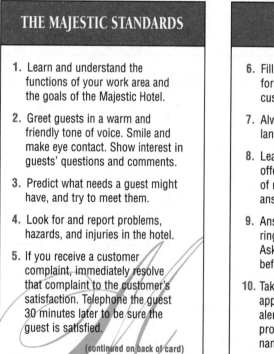

THE MAJESTIC STANDARDS

1. Learn and understand the functions of your work area and the goals of the Majestic Hotel.

2. Greet guests in a warm and friendly tone of voice. Smile and make eye contact. Show interest in guests' questions and comments.

3. Predict what needs a guest might have, and try to meet them.

4. Look for and report problems, hazards, and injuries in the hotel.

5. If you receive a customer complaint, immediately resolve that complaint to the customer's satisfaction. Telephone the guest 30 minutes later to be sure the guest is satisfied.

(continued on back of card)

6. Fill out a guest incident action form to communicate all customer complaints.

7. Always use positive and proper language.

8. Learn about the services Majestic offers (such as location and hours of restaurants) so that you can answer guests' questions.

9. Answer the telephone by the third ring. Use a pleasant tone of voice. Ask for a customer's permission before putting him or her on hold.

10. Take pride in your personal appearance. Stand tall and look alert. Wear spotless uniforms and proper shoes. Always wear your name tag.

1. Which of the following standards focus on communicating positive messages nonverbally?

   (1) standards 1 and 3
   (2) standards 4 and 6
   (3) standards 5 and 7
   (4) standards 2 and 10

2. Which of the following communication skills will be most helpful in meeting standard 9?

   (1) using positive facial expressions and gestures
   (2) sounding friendly and not interrupting the speaker
   (3) observing and understanding the gestures of others
   (4) understanding reasons for miscommunication and using problem-solving strategies

3. Briefly describe how Mai should greet guests in the gift shop.

   _____

   _____

TECH TIP

Mai's job includes answering the telephone in the gift shop. Mai has learned to start each conversation with a **salutation,** or greeting. Then she makes an identification statement, explaining who she is and what area of the hotel the caller has reached. Finally, she makes a **solicitation** statement, asking the caller to tell her how she may be of service.

Based on the Majestic service standards, write an effective telephone greeting for Mai that includes all three elements.

1. Salutation:

   _____

2. Identification:

   _____

3. Solicitation:

   _____

4. Describe the nonverbal communication skills Mai should use when answering the telephone.

   _____

Developing Effective Communication Skills

Miscommunication can cause problems for customers and employees alike. Some mistakes occur because people don't communicate clearly. Other problems occur because people act on their **prejudices,** or opinions formed without taking time to judge the situation at hand.

To be successful, you must learn to work with people of different races, cultures, and ages. Everybody you meet has different beliefs, feelings, and ways of doing things, because everybody **perceives,** or sees and interprets, the world differently. Treat all people equally and with respect.

Check each behavior that you currently do but would like to improve.

_____ 1. Not explaining something clearly

_____ 2. Not giving a full explanation

_____ 3. Not giving accurate details

_____ 4. Assuming something about a situation

_____ 5. Responding to your prejudices instead of to the person

_____ 6. Deliberately acting superior (or inferior) to someone

Finding Common Ground

Sometimes two people disagree because of differences in their backgrounds—where they grew up, what beliefs they have, how much education they have. Their experiences are so different that they can't understand each other's point of view. In these situations try putting yourself in the other person's shoes. Understanding the other person's viewpoint can help you to find common ground on which you can agree.

Which of the following is _not_ likely to help you understand another person's viewpoint?

(1) thinking about how the other person feels right now

(2) telling the person that his or her idea is bad

(3) asking the person what is needed to correct the situation

(4) putting yourself in the other person's place

Using Problem Solving

Misunderstandings with customers and clients cost a company money—and could cost you your job. Misunderstandings with co-workers also waste time and money and lead to tension in the workplace. So when problems occur, you must find a way to resolve them. The chart below gives tips for solving problems in different situations.

Problem-Solving Tips

When a misunderstanding occurs with a customer or a client:
- Apologize for the misunderstanding; admit any mistakes.
- Ask questions to be sure you understand the problem.
- Do not make negative comments; keep your attitude positive.
- Ask for the customer's advice in finding a solution that is good for both the customer and your business.

When a misunderstanding occurs with a co-worker:
- Be honest that there is a problem.
- Ask questions to be sure you both know what the problem is.
- Do not use language that attacks your co-worker personally.
- Work together to think of several possible solutions.
- Choose the solution that best meets both your needs.

Use the problem-solving tips above to answer the following questions.

1. Think of a misunderstanding you recently had with a customer, co-worker, or friend. Describe the misunderstanding.

   _____

   _____

   _____

2. How might you use the problem-solving tips in the chart to help resolve the problem? List the steps you plan to take.

   _____

   _____

   _____

WorkSkills

Service: Sherilyn is an African-American who works in a printing company. One of her co-workers, Gladys, likes to tell **ethnic** jokes, often about African-Americans. Sherilyn is insulted and angry at Gladys's insensitivity. Other workers have dropped hints that Gladys should stop telling ethnic jokes, but she hasn't gotten the point. Sherilyn and Gladys have to work together, so Sherilyn approaches Gladys in private to discuss the problem.

Communication Strategies

Read the dialogue below; then answer the questions on the next page.

Sherilyn: Gladys, why do you keep telling jokes that offend people?

Gladys: Which of my jokes have offended anyone?

Sherilyn: Just about all of them! I don't think your jokes about Blacks are funny. I feel humiliated and hurt by them.

Gladys: Geez, Sherilyn, lighten up. It's no big deal! I don't have to use Blacks in my jokes. I'll substitute some other group.

Sherilyn: First of all, it *is* a big deal. Secondly, no matter what group you substitute, someone is going to be offended.

Gladys: What's wrong with the jokes? I think they're funny!

Sherilyn: Gladys, I enjoy a good joke just as much as you do. But would you find it funny if I told jokes about your ethnic background?

Gladys: Well, no, I guess I wouldn't. I'm sorry, Sherilyn. Now I'm the one who's humiliated. I never meant to hurt you or anyone else. I guess I won't tell any more jokes.

Sherilyn: I'm not trying to keep you from telling all jokes, Gladys. You could just stop telling ethnic jokes. Maybe you could think more carefully about the jokes you're going to tell so you won't offend anyone.

Gladys: I should have done that to begin with. Thanks for being honest with me.

1. Describe four good points about the way Sherilyn handled the problem.

    a. _____

    b. _____

    c. _____

    d. _____

2. Describe two things that Sherilyn might have handled better.

    a. _____

    b. _____

3. Why didn't Sherilyn agree with the first solution Gladys offered?

    _____

    _____

    _____

4. Why didn't Sherilyn agree with the second solution Gladys offered?

    _____

    _____

5. What other solution did Sherilyn offer?

    _____

    _____

6. What did you learn about problem solving from this dialogue?

    _____

    _____

WRITE IT

Think about a time when a miscommunication occurred with a co-worker, a customer, or a neighbor because of a difference in experience or background. On a separate piece of paper, write a dialogue between you and the other person in which you try to resolve the problem. Be sure to:

- Tell what the problem is.
- Describe both points of view.
- Propose several possible solutions.
- Select one solution that meets everybody's needs.
- Explain why each of the other solutions is unacceptable.

Review

Reading about effective communication is only the first step toward becoming a better communicator. The next steps are to:

STEP 1: Apply the skills described.
STEP 2: Evaluate how well you did.
STEP 3: Make a personal "action plan" for developing effective communication skills in the future.

During the review that follows, you will take all three of these steps.

STEP 1: Apply Your Skills

The best place to apply effective work communication skills is, of course, at work itself. Think of a face-to-face business conversation you will have within the next few days, such as a work discussion with a supervisor or co-worker or a transaction with a customer. If you don't have a job right now, think of an upcoming "personal business" conversation, such as a discussion with a salesclerk to get information about a product you would like to buy, a parent-teacher conference, or an upcoming planning meeting with a member of a group you belong to.

On the lines below, describe the conversation you selected.

1.   Whom do you plan to talk to?

2.   When will you talk to this person?

3.   What is the purpose of the conversation?

4.   What would you like the outcome of the conversation to be?

Before you have the conversation, review the skills to practice.

During the conversation, you should:
- Practice effective speaking skills.
- Listen actively.
- Communicate a positive attitude through body language.

STEP 2: Self-Evaluation

1. After trying to apply effective communication skills, evaluate how well you did. Complete the following questionnaire as soon as possible after the conversation.

   During the conversation, I . . .

   Yes No
   ☐ ☐   **a.** Made an effort to speak clearly.
   ☐ ☐   **b.** Used a pleasant tone of voice.
   ☐ ☐   **c.** Remembered the purpose of the conversation and stuck to it.
   ☐ ☐   **d.** Noted and understood the other person's nonverbal "clues."
   ☐ ☐   **e.** Adjusted what I said to meet the other person's needs.
   ☐ ☐   **f.** Encouraged the other person to respond and ask questions.
   ☐ ☐   **g.** Smiled and used other positive nonverbal communication.
   ☐ ☐   **h.** Made eye contact with the person to show I was listening.
   ☐ ☐   **i.** Gave the other person my full attention.
   ☐ ☐   **j.** Asked questions when I didn't understand.
   ☐ ☐   **k.** Repeated important points or wrote them down.
   ☐ ☐   **l.** Treated the other person with respect.

2. Was the conversation successful? In other words, was the outcome what you hoped it would be? Explain why or why not.

   _____

   _____

3. Which skills do you think you applied particularly well? Why?

   _____

   _____

4. Which skills would you like to practice further? Why?

   _____

   _____

STEP 3: Personal Action Plan

An action plan is a list of steps you take to reach a goal. In this case, your goal is to take what you learned from the self-evaluation, plan how to be a better communicator, and evaluate your progress over the next two weeks.

Answer these questions to make your plan and assess your progress.

1. **Which communication skills do you most need to develop?** Review the self-evaluation you completed on page 29, and choose two or three skills. If necessary, talk over your choices with someone else, or complete the questionnaire on page 29 from the other person's viewpoint.

   I need to develop the following communication skills:

   _____

2. **Over what period will you work at improving these skills?** Choose ten days in the near future.

   I will work to improve these skills from _____ to _____.

3. **What will you do to develop the skills you choose?** Be specific. Review this lesson and the list at the bottom of page 28; then write down what you plan to do in future conversations.

   In my conversations, I will

   _____

4. **How will you measure your progress?** You can use the questionnaire on page 29 to evaluate the conversations you have each day. Or you might discuss your plan with a co-worker or friend, and ask the person to help you evaluate your progress. A third way is to keep a "communication journal" by noting what communications did and did not go well each day.

   I will keep track of my progress by

   _____

5. **How will you evaluate what you learned during the two weeks?** As a final step, evaluate what you learned. Ask yourself, "What am I doing now that I did not do in the past? What are the positive effects of my efforts?"

   By following the action plan, I learned to

   _____

BEFORE you WATCH

program **10**

WATCH

Communicating with Co-Workers and Supervisors

In the video program you are about to watch, you will see **strategies** employees use to communicate effectively with each other and with their supervisors. You will also see good ways to settle disagreements.

While you watch the video, notice specific steps people take to communicate well and resolve **conflicts.**

In your personal life, you may communicate for many reasons. You may want to chat with a friend, order a carry-out dinner, or find out what your child's day was like. At work, the main reason to communicate is to exchange information. Co-workers and supervisors communicate to find out about projects, check each other's work, and solve problems. Whether you are at home or at work, effective communication strategies can help you "get your message across."

Sneak Preview

This exercise previews some of the concepts from Program 10. After you answer the questions, use the Feedback on page 33 to help set your learning goals.

CONSTRUCTION: You are the supervisor for an independent plumbing contractor. Your company was called to investigate a leak in the basement of an old office building. While discussing the problem with the building operations manager, you notice Raiz, one of your new workers. He has removed part of the false ceiling in the basement and has his head and arms up inside the ceiling, busily working. You quickly finish your conversation.

You: Whoa, Raiz. What are you doing?

Raiz: I was just about to unwrap the insulation so we can see where the leak is coming from.

You: Don't touch the insulation, Raiz. Do you know what's inside it?

Raiz: No... Not exactly.

You: Well, that's what I was trying to find out from the operations manager. Old buildings like this one usually have asbestos in the insulation. And the government has strict safety regulations about how materials containing asbestos are to be removed. If asbestos fibers get into the air, it's dangerous for you, your co-workers, and the tenants.

Raiz: I'm sorry! I was just eager to start. You stopped me just in time.

You: I'm glad you're eager, Raiz. But you should have talked with me first. Or I probably should have said something earlier. The point is that part of my job is to check out the work site for my crew. If something goes wrong on a job, it's my fault. So next time wait until I have a chance to check out the situation and give you instructions. Then you can do a good job without any problems. Any questions?

Raiz: Not right now... But I'll be sure to ask when I do. Thanks, Boss.

Write *True* if the statement is true; *False* if it is false.

_____ 1. Your communications with the operations manager and Raiz had little to do with the job.

_____ 2. When you saw Raiz working, you suspected a problem and reacted appropriately.

_____ 3. Raiz's response "You stopped me just in time" shows that he understood what you said about handling asbestos.

_____ 4. You made the comment "So next time wait until I... give you instructions" to show Raiz who's boss.

_____ 5. By saying, "I probably should have said something earlier," you were letting Raiz know that the miscommunication was partly your fault.

_____ 6. You never came up with a plan of action to help Raiz know when to start a job.

Feedback for Sneak Preview

- If you got all of the answers right . . .   you have a basic understanding of how to communicate with co-workers and supervisors. In the video, focus on how to communicate effectively with difficult supervisors and co-workers.

- If you missed question 1 or 2 . . .   you need to work on how to communicate successfully with co-workers.

- If you missed question 3 or 4 . . .   you need to work on how to communicate successfully with supervisors.

- If you missed question 5 or 6 . . .   you need to work on resolving conflicts with co-workers and supervisors.

Answers for Sneak Preview:
1. False 2. True 3. True 4. False 5. True 6. False

Vocabulary for *Communicating with Co-Workers and Supervisors*

conflict resolution	the settling of disagreements by finding common goals
conflicts	disagreements between people who have different goals
feedback	an evaluation of an action or process, such as feedback a supervisor gives to employees about their work
priorities	tasks that are the most important or that must be done first
procedures	guidelines or rules for doing a job
strategies	effective ways of getting something done

Now watch Program 10.

After you watch, work on:
- pages 35–50 in this workbook
- Internet activities at www.pbs.org/literacy

AFTER you WATCH

program **10**

Communicating with Co-Workers and Supervisors

On the following pages, you will learn more about the ideas discussed in the video program and have an opportunity to develop your skills.

Think About the Key Points from the Video Program

When communicating with co-workers, your employer expects you to:
- Exchange job-related information.
- Keep workplace communications on task.

When communicating with supervisors, you need to:
- Use active listening strategies to understand instructions.
- Take responsibility for your work.

When resolving conflicts at work, you need to:
- Use problem-solving skills to identify the cause of the problem.
- Take steps to make sure problems don't recur.

WORKTIP

When you know you will be exchanging information with a co-worker or supervisor at a later time:
- Jot down notes about points you want to discuss.
- Gather items such as bills, letters, or your calendar that you will need to communicate clearly.
- Be on time for the meeting.

Communicating Successfully with Co-Workers

The video program showed different situations in which employees communicate with each other. Why is work communication so important? When employees are careful to exchange information, the workplace is productive and organized. Time is saved, and mistakes are avoided. People also get along better because no one feels "left in the dark." All in all, life is easier when you communicate well with co-workers.

Note that being a good communicator doesn't mean you have to avoid all social conversations. In most cases, social conversations are OK. They help co-workers get to know and care about each other. They also take the edge off a busy day. Just be sure your chats never interfere with your work.

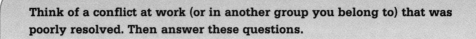

Check off all the reasons you communicated today with a co-worker or with someone to conduct personal business.

- ☐ Job information
- ☐ Social conversation
- ☐ Conflict resolution
- ☐ Job feedback

- ☐ Instructions
- ☐ Job training
- ☐ Work progress
- ☐ Job evaluation

- ☐ Deadlines
- ☐ Absence
- ☐ Planning
- ☐ Problem solving

Using Good Judgment

How should you settle disagreements with co-workers? In the video program, you saw effective techniques to think through and resolve a difficult work situation. Show good judgment by staying positive and getting co-workers to work on the problem rather than complain about a supervisor. If you need help with **conflict resolution,** what do you do? A manager may have the power to enforce a quick solution, but your co-worker may resent having no voice in the solution—and take that anger out on you. Weigh the pros and cons of any action. Then go with your best judgment.

Think of a conflict at work (or in another group you belong to) that was poorly resolved. Then answer these questions.

1. How was the conflict resolved?

_____

2. What might you have done to resolve the conflict more successfully?

_____

_____

Keeping Workplace Communication on Task

Have a co-worker's thoughts ever seemed to wander while you spoke? Have you ever been talking to a co-worker only to hear the person say "Huh?" At work, you need to help your co-workers focus on your message—and stay focused. Try the following tips.

Tips for Focusing

1. **Start the communication by asking a question.**
   Don't continue until the listener answers.

2. **Keep the communication simple and direct.**
   Match your language to the listener's understanding.

3. **Present the main points in a clear order.**
   Use signals such as _First, Next, The most important..._

4. **Constantly check to see that your co-worker is listening and understanding.**
   Watch the listener's facial expressions and gestures.
   Ask questions; encourage the listener to ask questions.

Read each part of the conversation below. Then write the number(s) of the tips above that apply to each part. Some tips will be used more than once.

_____ **1.** "Jeff," says Pat. "Could you help me convert a computer file?" Jeff smiles and nods.
_____ **2.** He looks at the computer screen and says, "First, you need to open the conversion application. Just click up here. Next, you open the file you want to convert. To do that, click on 'Open.' That's it. Now, the computer is asking if you want to convert. Click on 'Yes.' Finally, do a 'Save as.'" _____ **3.** Jeff, noticing Pat's blank look, says, "Do you know how to 'Save as'?" Pat shakes her head. _____ **4.** Jeff says, "When you do a 'Save as,' you tell the computer what program to save the file in. Don't bother to read all the programs listed. We use WordPerfect, so just click on that." _____ **5.** Jeff, noting Pat's nervous smile, says, "See? The file's converted and saved. You did fine. Any other questions?"

HEALTH CARE: Juanita is a nurse's aide at Villa Health Care Center. She worked the night shift for more than a year before an opening came up on days. Juanita moved to the day shift to spend more time with her son.

During the two months that Juanita has worked days, Zoya, an aide from the night shift, has asked her to switch shifts three times because of "scheduling problems." Juanita worked those three nights, hoping that Zoya would be willing to return the favor when she needed it. Juanita's son has asked her to be a parent helper for his school field trip next Thursday.

Communication Strategies

With a partner, choose roles, one of you playing Juanita and the other playing Zoya. Read each set of statements that follow. Then use the communication strategies of *using good judgment* and *keeping workplace communications on task* to select the statement in each set that will lead to good communication between Juanita and Zoya.

Juanita:

- Guess what, Zoya? You're going to work my day shift next Thursday!
- Zoya, would you be able to switch shifts with me next Thursday so I can go with my son on a field trip?
- Hi, Zoya! I'm going on a field trip next Thursday with my son.

Zoya:

- Really? Where are you going?
- Gee, that's the day Jim and I are going to the Cubs game.
- No way. I can't.

Write your choice here:

1. _____

   _____

   _____

   _____

2. _____

   _____

   _____

   _____

Juanita:
- Come on, Zoya. You owe me three shift changes!
- Could you go to a game on Wednesday or Friday instead?
- The school's taking the fourth graders to the Museum of Science and Industry.

3. _____
_____
_____
_____

Zoya:
- I doubt it. Jim's already asked for the day off.
- Hey, I don't owe you anything!
- Wow! That's the neatest museum in the city.

4. _____
_____
_____
_____

Juanita:
- Can you do it for me?
- Please, Zoya. How many times have I switched shifts for you?
- If you don't switch shifts with me, I'm going to our supervisor.

5. _____
_____
_____
_____

Zoya:
- Go ahead, but you'll be sorry.
- You're right. You've always been there when I needed to switch.
- Can I do what?

6. _____
_____
_____
_____

Juanita:
- Thanks, Zoya! I really appreciate it!
- Can you switch shifts with me so I can go on the field trip?
- No. You're the one who will be sorry!

7. _____
_____
_____
_____

WRITE IT ··

Imagine Zoya refused to help. What should Juanita do? On a separate piece of paper, write down two possible solutions to the problem. Then list the pros and cons of each solution. Which is the better solution? Why?

Communicating with Supervisors

As you saw in the video program, employees and supervisors need to communicate to exchange work information. Employees need to let their supervisor know if work is "on track" or if there is a problem. Supervisors need to explain work rules and **procedures**—and give employees **feedback** about their work. *Both* supervisors and employees are responsible for the success of their communication. Make sure you do your part. If you aren't getting the information you need, ask questions. If a problem occurs, talk about it. If communication isn't going well, take responsibility for making it better.

Answer these questions.

1. List five reasons you communicated with your supervisor (or someone to handle personal business) this week.

   a. _____

   b. _____

   c. _____

   d. _____

   e. _____

2. What can you do to communicate better in the future?

   _____

   _____

   _____

   _____

   _____

Taking Direction

As a student, you listened to directions from your teachers. When you didn't listen carefully, you probably made mistakes—and learned to listen more carefully.

As an adult in the working world, you are expected to listen carefully to instructions about how to do a job, to use equipment, or to figure out **priorities.** How can you listen better to instructions? Follow the tips on the next page.

Active Listening Strategies

- Listen for the purpose of the communication.
- Take brief notes about the steps in a job or work that needs to be done.
- Listen for words that tell the order of steps (*first, next, then, finally*).
- Ask questions if you're not sure what to do.
- Repeat important facts so the other person knows you understand.

Think of a time this week when you listened to directions.

1. Check off each active listening strategy you used.

   ☐ Listened for the purpose of the communication.
   ☐ Listened for words that told the order of steps or points.
   ☐ Asked questions when not sure what to do.
   ☐ Took brief notes about the steps.
   ☐ Repeated the most important facts.

2. What new listening strategies will you use next time? Why?

Responding to Feedback

Have you ever watched coaches give feedback to their players? Even in the heat of games, players listen carefully and keep their cool. That's because they know the purpose of feedback: to help them reach excellence. Take a tip from the sports stars. When supervisors give you feedback—informally on the work floor or formally in a job review—remember that the purpose is to improve your work. Listen carefully, and don't take criticism personally. Show that you understand by making the changes your supervisors suggest. When you receive feedback in the positive way it is intended, you learn how to be your best.

Write *True* if the statement is true; *False* if it is false.

_____ 1. Supervisors criticize workers to show them who's boss.

_____ 2. Feedback is meant to help people improve their work.

_____ 3. People who ignore feedback may not improve.

_____ 4. People should actively listen when receiving feedback.

SERVICE: Charlie is an order clerk for Nuland Kitchen Appliance Distributor. He just received a telephone call from a dealer who wants to order $32,000 worth of stoves, refrigerators, and dishwashers. A recent memo from Nuland's owner, Rafael, warned the order clerks to get his approval before placing an order from this dealer. Charlie is nervous about going to Rafael because he has been in a bad mood all day.

Communication Strategies

Read the dialogue below, and answer the questions that follow.

Charlie: Uh, excuse me, Rafael?

Rafael: Charlie, if this isn't important, please wait until later.

Charlie: I think you want to know about this. I've got a $32,000 order to place.

Rafael: That's great. But why bother me? You know what to do.

Charlie: Well, yes, normally I do, but you sent the order clerks a memo telling us to get your approval before placing an order from Trucko Brothers

Rafael: Well, why didn't you tell me it was from Trucko Brothers? They still owe us $17,000 on their last order! Call them back and tell them we need a check for $10,000 by the end of the week before we can place the order.

Charlie: [*Writing a note to himself*] OK, if we get a $10,000 check by the end of the week, then I can place this new order, right?

Rafael: That's right. And thanks for checking with me. You were right. I did want to know about this order. I'm sorry... I'm just buried with last minute details for the new showroom.

Charlie: No problem. I'll make that call to Trucko Brothers now.

1. The reason Charlie communicated with his supervisor was to

    (1) give information about the order clerks

    (2) tell the supervisor that his moodiness scares the employees

    (3) get approval for a new order from Trucko Brothers

    (4) ask why Trucko Brothers hasn't paid its bill

2. Rafael thought Charlie was bothering him unnecessarily because

   (1) Rafael was too busy to listen to Charlie's explanation
   (2) Charlie had never communicated with Rafael before
   (3) Rafael was working on the new showroom
   (4) Charlie did not explain right away whom the order was from

3. Which of the following statements shows that Charlie was practicing the active listening strategy of repeating important points?

   (1) "Uh, excuse me, Rafael?"
   (2) "I think you want to know about this."
   (3) "Well, yes, normally I do."
   (4) "OK, if we get a $10,000 check by the end of the week, then I can place this new order, right?"

4. Charlie wrote himself a note to

   (1) show Rafael he was sorry for interrupting him
   (2) remember the instructions Rafael gave him
   (3) help Rafael with the new showroom
   (4) plan what to tell the other order clerks

5. What feedback did Rafael give to Charlie at the end of the conversation?

   (1) He did a good job.
   (2) He took Rafael's comments too personally.
   (3) He needed to take responsibility for his work.
   (4) He needed to listen more carefully.

6. Which of the following communication strategies did Charlie *not* use?

   (1) Stay focused on the purpose of the communication.
   (2) Start the communication by asking a question.
   (3) Present the main points in a clear order.
   (4) Don't take constructive criticism personally.

MATH MATTERS

Reread the dialogue between Charlie and Rafael. How much will Trucko Brothers owe Nuland Kitchen Appliance Distributor on both orders after paying $10,000? Show how you got your answer.

_____

_____

_____

Resolving Conflicts with Co-Workers and Supervisors

Conflict is a normal part of every workplace. The challenge is learning how to deal with conflict effectively. In the video, workers used several good communication strategies to resolve conflicts they were experiencing. When resolving work conflicts, try to see the problem as a work problem rather than as a personal problem, act quickly to resolve the problem, use active listening skills, stay calm, and focus on the work to be done.

Remember, the main goal in resolving conflicts with co-workers and supervisors is to correct the problem so work can be done. Therefore, the first step to take is to *identify the problem.* Ask good questions to find out what the problem is. Then think about the cause of the problem. Is it caused by differences in personalities and work habits? Or is it caused by factors in the workplace that can be changed for the better?

1. List two conflicts you have had recently with co-workers, supervisors, or friends.

    a. _____

    b. _____

2. What was the problem in each conflict?

    a. _____

    b. _____

3. Was each problem caused by a difference in personalities and work habits, or by some other factor?

    a. _____

    b. _____

Developing Strategies to Resolve Conflicts

What's the best way to resolve a conflict after you have identified the problem? No single way is best, because the factors surrounding each problem will be different. The chart on the next page lists conflict resolution strategies that will help you evaluate each problem.

Conflict Resolution Strategies

1. **Don't let the problem get personal.**
   Stay focused on both parties' mutual goal—to get the job done.

2. **Develop two or more plans of action.**
   List the pros and cons of each plan; then choose the best plan.

3. **Resolve the conflict.**
   Put your plan into effect.

4. **Ensure that the problem won't happen again.**
   Make any changes in the workplace that are needed.

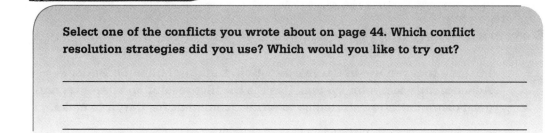

Select one of the conflicts you wrote about on page 44. Which conflict resolution strategies did you use? Which would you like to try out?

_____

_____

_____

Developing Strategies for Difficult Situations

Sometimes conflicts occur with difficult co-workers or supervisors. To communicate effectively with difficult people, keep these points in mind:

- A person's age, gender, race, culture, and work experience may affect the way he or she sees a situation.
- Although it's nice to be friends with co-workers and supervisors, don't let your friendship affect your work or the way you handle a conflict.
- Take responsibility for any misunderstanding that you may have caused.
- Always use words and behavior that show your professionalism.

Give an example of a time when you didn't see eye to eye with someone. What were the reasons you disagreed or misunderstood each other? How did you resolve the problem? What might you do differently?

_____

_____

_____

SERVICE: Caryn is a thirty-one-year-old worker with ten years of experience in collections. She has worked at National Adjustment Corporation for three years. She is training Lillian, who is fifty-four years old. Like Caryn, Lillian has ten years of experience in collections, but she has been out of the workforce for the past fifteen years. When Lillian last worked as a collector, she would go to a file cabinet, pull a debtor's file, return to her desk, call the debtor, make handwritten notes in the file, and return the file to the cabinet. National Adjustment doesn't keep paper files on its debtors anymore. Now the collectors work on-line, entering on their computers any information about calls to debtors. The computer system is quicker and more accurate than the old way of doing collections.

Communication Strategies

Imagine that you are in Caryn's situation, training Lillian on National Adjustment's computer system. Use the conflict resolution strategies and good communication strategies to write a comment for Caryn to make.

Lillian: You won't have to spend much time with me, Caryn. I've probably got more experience than you. I was a collector for ten years before I left the workforce.

Caryn: [*Example*]: *Yes, I know. Just let me point out a few things in the computer system.*

Caryn: Press F3 to get into the comment section. Now you can read any comments that have already been entered about this debt.

Lillian: Who wrote these comments? She could use a few lessons in writing clearly!

1. **Caryn:** _____
   _____
   _____

Caryn: Each time you call the debtor, you should make a note about what happened. Use the arrow keys to move the cursor to the top line of the comment section.

Lillian: Caryn, you don't have to tell me to write a comment. I've done this before! But it would be faster for me to just pull the debtor's paper file and make my notes there.

2. **Caryn:**_____

_____

_____

Caryn: To send a form letter to the debtor, press F7 and select a letter from the list.

Lillian: I've never sent out a form letter before, and I'm not going to start now.

3. **Caryn:**_____

_____

_____

Caryn: Lillian, I think we have a problem that we should talk about.

Lillian: And just what do you think the problem is, Caryn?

4. **Caryn:**_____

_____

_____

Caryn: Do you think we can try to work this out?

Lillian: Maybe. What do you have in mind?

5. **Caryn:**_____

_____

_____

READ IT

Many popular magazines for businesspeople give tips on how to work out problems with co-workers. Find some tips in a magazine at the library. On a separate piece of paper, write down tips you'd like to try and share.

Review

Reading about effective communication is only the first step toward becoming a better communicator. The next steps are to:

STEP 1: Apply the skills described.
STEP 2: Evaluate how well you did.
STEP 3: Make a personal "action plan."

During the review that follows, you will take all three of these steps.

STEP 1: Apply Your Skills (within the next few days)

The best place to apply effective work communication skills is, of course, at work itself. Think of a face-to-face business conversation you will have within the next few days with a supervisor or co-worker. If you don't have a job right now, think of an upcoming "personal business" conversation, such as a discussion with a salesclerk to get information about a product you want to buy or a parent-teacher conference at your child's school.

On the lines below, describe the conversation you selected.

1. Whom do you plan to talk to?

   _____

2. When will you talk to this person?

   _____

3. What is the purpose of the conversation?

   _____

4. What would you like the outcome of the conversation to be?

   _____

During the conversation, you will practice:

- Keeping the communication on task.
- Listening carefully to directions, instructions, and feedback.
- Using problem-solving strategies.

Review the skills you should apply. Read the Listening and Speaking Checklists on page 190 and the Problem-Solving Checklists on pages 188–189.

STEP 2: Self-Evaluation (right after the conversation)

Evaluate how well you applied the communication skills. Complete the following questionnaire as soon after the conversation as possible.

1. During the conversation, I . . .

   Yes No
   □ □ **a.** Started the conversation by asking a question.
   □ □ **b.** Kept the communication simple and direct.
   □ □ **c.** Presented the main points in a clear order.
   □ □ **d.** Kept the communication on task.
   □ □ **e.** Looked for clues that the person was listening and understanding.
   □ □ **f.** Asked questions when I needed more information.
   □ □ **g.** Encouraged the other person to ask questions.
   □ □ **h.** Actively listened to feedback and instructions.
   □ □ **i.** Used good judgment in resolving a conflict.
   □ □ **j.** Asked good questions to identify any problems.
   □ □ **k.** Used conflict resolution tips to solve problems.
   □ □ **l.** Saw problems from the other person's viewpoint.

2. Was the conversation successful? In other words, was the outcome what you hoped it would be? Explain why or why not.

   _____

3. Which skills do you think you applied particularly well? Why?

   _____

4. Which skills would you like to practice further? Why?

   _____

STEP 3: Personal Action Plan (over the next two weeks)

An action plan is a series of steps you take to reach a goal. In this case, your goal is to take what you learned from the self-evaluation, plan how to be a better communicator, and evaluate your progress over the next two weeks.

Answer these questions to make your plan and assess your progress.

1. **Which communication skills do you most need to develop?** Review the self-evaluation you completed on page 49, and choose two or three skills that you answered *No* to. If necessary, talk your choices over with a supervisor or friend. Or complete the self-evaluation again, only this time imagine how the other person would evaluate you.

    I need to develop the following communication skills:

    _____

2. **Over what period will you work at improving these skills?** (Choose ten days in the near future.)

    I will work to improve these skills from _____ to _____.

3. **What will you do to develop the skills you choose?** Be specific. Review this unit and the Checklists on pages 188–190; then write down what you plan to do in future conversations.

    In my business conversations, I will

    _____

4. **How will you measure your progress?** One way is to use the questionnaire on page 49 to evaluate the conversations you have each day. Another way is to discuss your plan with a co-worker and ask the person to help you evaluate your progress. Or keep a "communication journal" by noting what did and did not go well each day.

    I will keep track of my progress by

    _____

5. **How will you evaluate what you learned during the two weeks?** As a final step, evaluate what you learned. Ask yourself, "What am I doing now that I didn't do before? What are the positive effects of my efforts?"

    By following the action plan, I learned to

    _____

BEFORE you WATCH

program **11**

WATCH

Working Together

OBJECTIVES

In this lesson, you will work with the following concepts and skills:

1. Learning to do work as part of a team
2. Solving problems as a team member
3. Acting as part of an effective team

The video program you are about to watch shows the importance of teamwork—cooperation among employees to meet individual and group work **goals.** You will learn the purpose and pluses of teamwork. You also will learn how to be an effective **team** member.

As you watch the video, notice how team members do their work. Pay close attention to the strategies that team members use to get along with each other. And note the **leadership** qualities every team member has.

Although teamwork is important to job success, it's helpful off the job, too. Parents and teachers use teamwork to help children succeed in school. Families use teamwork to support each other and finish housework. Neighbors use teamwork to solve common problems and improve their communities. In fact, whenever you work with others to meet a common goal, you need teamwork skills.

Sneak Preview

This exercise previews some of the concepts from Program 11. After you answer the questions, use the Feedback on page 53 to help set your learning goals.

SERVICE: Today is "Take a Student to Work Day" at Spree Airlines. You are a ground service manager explaining to Ed, an eighth grader, how teamwork helps ground services ensure that jets leave on schedule.

You: Once a plane arrives at the gate, we have 30 minutes to get it ready.

Ed: All you have to do is unload and load baggage, right?

You: That's only part of our job, Ed.

Ed: What else do you do?

You: Well, we coordinate with food services so their truck and our baggage trailers don't try to service the plane at the same time. We secure everything in the hold—the compartment where the baggage is stored—and make sure the weight of the cargo, or other packages, is OK.

Ed: What happens if there's too much weight?

You: We remove some bags and cargo. We also let the pilot know.

Ed: Cool! I didn't know you got to talk with the pilot!

You: Sure. We talk with the pilots, mechanics, customer service clerks, and flight attendants any time we see a problem. Earlier, I had trouble locking a cargo hold door on a plane. I called the pilot to let her know the flight might be delayed. Then I called the mechanics so they could fix the lock. Also, flight attendants call us about last-minute luggage.

Ed: You mean if someone gets to the airport late?

You: Yes, but also when the overhead compartments are full. Then we pick up the extra carry-on bags and put them in the hold.

Ed: Who's in charge of putting fuel in the plane?

You: We are. And if it's cold outside, we also de-ice the plane.

Ed: Wow! I can't believe it all gets done in 30 minutes!

Answer these questions based on the situation described above.

1. What common goal do the ground services of Spree Airlines have?

    _____

2. List three examples of teamwork among ground services groups.

    a. _____

    b. _____

    c. _____

3. List three jobs the ground services team does.

a. _____

b. _____

c. _____

4. Do you think the ground services team of Spree Airlines functions as a successful team? Why or why not?

_____

_____

_____

Feedback for Sneak Preview

- If you got all of the answers right . . .

  you have a basic understanding of the teamwork approach to work. In the video, focus on the skills needed to become an effective team member.

- If you missed question 1 or 2 . . .

  you need to learn how to develop teamwork skills.

- If you missed question 3 . . .

  you need to learn how people participate on a work team.

- If you missed question 4 . . .

  you need to work on the skills needed to be part of an effective team.

Vocabulary for *Working Together*

alternative	a choice from among two or more things
committees	groups, often temporary, that are formed to solve a specific problem or meet a specific goal
diversity	variety; differences
goals	objectives or desired outcomes
initiative	self-motivation; effort to solve a work problem or improve work methods
interpersonal	between persons, as in interpersonal communication skills
leadership	guiding and directing others
motivate	to provide with an incentive or other reason to take action
team	a group of people working together to meet a common goal

PBS **LiteracyLink**®

Now watch Program 11.

After you watch, work on:
- pages 55–70 in this workbook
- Internet activities at www.pbs.org/literacy

AFTER you WATCH

Working Together

On the following pages, you will learn more about the issues discussed in the video program and have an opportunity to develop your skills.

Think About the Key Points from the Video Program

When you are developing teamwork skills, an employer expects you to:

- Learn from and teach co-workers.
- Approach a task as a team player.

When working as part of a team, you need to:

- Understand and respect the team's common goal.
- Share responsibility for meeting the team's goal.

To be a team player, you need to:

- Develop **interpersonal** skills that will help the team.
- Work cooperatively with other team members.

WORKTIP

When you are working as part of a team:

- Listen actively to your team members.
- Trust and respect team members and their ideas.
- Stay on task; don't get distracted from team goals.

Developing Teamwork Skills

In the video program, you saw employees sharing their knowledge, ideas, experience, and viewpoints to meet common goals and solve problems. Why is teamwork good for business? When employees work together, they learn from each other. More work gets done—and it gets done faster and better because everyone contributes ideas and effort. Businesses run more smoothly, and customers are happier. With teamwork, everyone wins.

Evaluate your experience as a member of a team at work, in sports, or in the community. Write *True* if the statement is true; *False* if it is false. Then think about how you could become a better team member.

_____ 1. Everyone on the team contributed to the team effort.

_____ 2. I felt a sense of responsibility to help my teammates.

_____ 3. My teammates and I cooperated rather than competed.

_____ 4. I felt I was an important member of the team.

_____ 5. My teammates motivated me to overcome difficulties.

Approaching a Task as a Team Player

Working as a member of a team is different from doing work alone. How can you approach tasks as a team player? Follow the six steps below.

Six Steps to the Teamwork Approach

1. Understand the task or problem; ask questions or do research.

2. Discuss the task or problem with others.

3. Develop a plan of action or **alternative** plans.

4. Consider the pros and cons of each plan.

5. Communicate the plan to others and put it into effect.

6. Together, evaluate the outcome; make necessary changes.

Write *Yes* if the statement describes a teamwork approach, *No* if it does not.

_____ 1. You struggle with a problem, afraid to ask others for help.

_____ 2. You come up with a plan and put it into effect by yourself.

_____ 3. You ask co-workers and others for suggestions.

_____ 4. Others learn of your plan only after you put it into effect.

_____ 5. You make changes to the plan after it's in effect without consulting others.

Building a Teamwork Approach

How can you build skills in approaching work as part of a team?

- *Learn to relate to others.* Try to see the good in ideas that are different from yours. If you disagree, give reasons, and state them in a positive way.
- *Take the **initiative**.* Speak up when there's a problem—and be ready to offer solutions that meet group goals.
- *Help to build general agreement.* Don't insist on having your way. Help the team find and meet a common goal.
- *Be upbeat.* A little encouragement can energize the whole team.

Evaluate your teamwork qualities. Rank your teamwork qualities in order from strongest to weakest. Then think about how to strengthen your weaker qualities.

Teamwork Strengths

My strongest qualities	
My weakest quality	

SERVICE: As the customer service representative of a small quick-print shop, Waddell greets customers and talks with them about their printing needs. He listens and asks questions to be sure he understands what they want. Then he writes up the printing orders on a sheet of paper for the press people, who actually do the job. In the past, Waddell carried each order into the press room in the back of the shop and discussed the order with a press person. But a month ago, the press room was moved out of the quick-print shop to another location. Now, Waddell keeps the customers' orders until the end of the day. Then he uses a messenger service to deliver all the orders to the press before he closes up shop. The press people work three shifts to keep the presses running 24 hours a day. They usually begin Waddell's orders in the middle of the night. Since the new system was put into effect, Waddell has received complaints from customers about orders being done incorrectly or coming back late.

Communication Strategies

Read the conversation between Waddell and Joe, the press supervisor. Then use the "Six Steps to the Teamwork Approach" on page 56 to answer the questions that follow.

"Joe, the number of jobs with printing errors has almost doubled since the presses were moved," says Waddell. "What's the problem?"

"Well, I think the biggest problem is a lack of communication," Joe suggests. "Sometimes the work orders we get aren't clear. The press person doesn't want to wake you in the middle of the night with questions. So the job either gets done incorrectly or just sits until morning, when the press person can talk with you. Any job that waits until morning has to be completed the next day, which backs up every other job we had scheduled for that day. Either way, it takes longer to do our work—and that cuts into the business's profits."

1. How did Waddell apply steps 1 and 2 in this situation?

_____

_____

2. What plans of action can you think of to help solve the problem (step 3)?

_____

_____

_____

Here are a few of Waddell and Joe's ideas:

- Call Waddell with questions anytime during the day or night.
- Pay extra to have a messenger service deliver orders four times a day.
- Make an order form that is easier for the press people to understand.
- Don't print any jobs that a press person has questions about.

3. Now put step 4 of the teamwork approach into effect. Which plan, including your own, will do the most to prevent mistakes and to save time and money? Explain.

_____

_____

_____

4. How might Waddell and Joe carry out step 5? Who will do what?

_____

_____

_____

5. How will Waddell and Joe know if their plan solved the problem (step 6)?

_____

_____

TECH TIP

Some businesses use fax machines to send orders. These machines send written messages over telephone lines almost instantly. Orders may also be sent quickly with a computer by e-mail. Which of these methods do you think Waddell and Joe should use? Why?

_____

_____

_____

Participating on a Work Team

In the video program, you saw problems that occurred when communication broke down between team members. Sometimes people work as part of a group, but the group does not work as a team. Maybe a supervisor does not show good leadership skills. Or perhaps co-workers perform their individual jobs, but none of them communicates well with each other. If you find yourself in a similar work situation, you may need to take the **initiative,** or first step. Use the teamwork skills you have learned to develop a plan to help your group become a team.

> Write *Team* if the statement describes a team skill, *Group* if it describes the behavior of a group that is not a team.
>
> _____ 1. You keep your opinions to yourself.
> _____ 2. You show respect for others.
> _____ 3. You follow through on promised actions.
> _____ 4. You blame others for problems.
> _____ 5. You help settle misunderstandings.

Participating on an Organized Work Team

Sometimes employers organize **committees,** or special teams, to work on a specific problem or goal. For example, a safety committee might be organized to find ways to reduce accidents and make the workplace healthier. The special team develops a plan of action, assigns tasks to each team member, and then puts the plan into effect. Everyone on the team shares responsibility for the outcome, regardless of whether the plan succeeds or fails. As with a sports team, everyone does his or her part to meet the team goal. And everyone supports each other, win or lose.

> **Think of five ways in which a work team is like a sports team. Then complete the chart on page 61.**

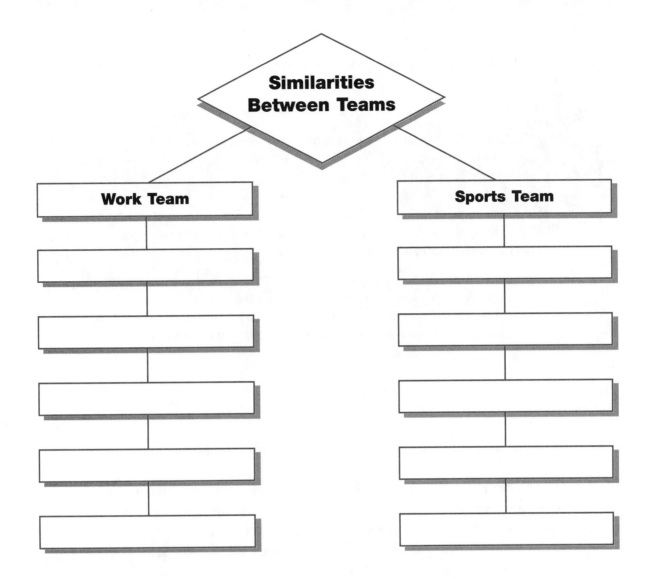

Similarities Between Teams

Work Team

Sports Team

Sharing Responsibility for the Outcome

No one person knows all the right answers. That's why a team effort can be more effective than an individual one. But to be effective, team members must take responsibility for meeting team goals. As a member of a team, you are responsible for identifying what is needed to make the team successful. You are responsible for suggesting ideas, giving information, and sharing in the tasks identified by the team. That doesn't mean you work alone or try to run the show. It means you and your teammates help each other put the team's ideas into effect and check the team's progress. Successful team members give each other positive feedback and find ways to improve the team's plan. In this way, every team member has a chance to learn management skills. Don't waste your chance!

> Think of a group you might help. The group might be a committee or other work team, or it might be a school, community, or religious group. On a separate piece of paper, list five skills, ideas, or resources you might add to the group.

MANUFACTURING: Jesse is a precision assembler in a factory that produces sports utility vehicles. His job is to install splash shields, rods, and assorted screws in the rear ends of vehicles that move along the assembly line. Jesse has been asked to join a committee of three other production workers to improve the safety and health conditions for assembly line workers. This is the first time the company has asked workers to contribute ideas.

A supervisor explains the committee's goal: to find ways to improve safety conditions along the assembly line. He gives committee members a budget. The committee must decide what changes they can afford to make and how to put them into effect. The committee will then submit their proposals for management's OK.

Communication Strategies

Read the committee conversation below. Then answer the questions on the next page.

"What the heck is this about?" grumbles Maurice. "I've been here for eight years, and management has always told me what to do and when to do it. Now they expect me to do their thinking for them. I don't get it!"

"Me either," adds Max. "I don't get paid to make decisions. Besides, how are we supposed to know what safety changes to make?"

"Let's think about this," suggests Jesse. "All of us are uneasy about making decisions that will affect our co-workers. But maybe management has finally realized that we know more about safety issues than they do."

"That's true," adds Consuela. "We're the ones who deal with the dangers on the line each day. I think we can come up with good ideas."

"Yeah, but if we start making the decisions, our co-workers are going to accuse us of being chummy with management," warns Maurice.

"Not if we ask them for their opinions and suggestions," says Jesse.

"Maybe we could put together a questionnaire for everyone to fill out," suggests Consuela. "That way, everyone could make suggestions."

"That's not a bad idea," Max responds. "Our decisions would be a little easier to make—and to live with! I say we write up this questionnaire now, before I have a change of heart. Agreed?"

"Yep!" "Fine by me!" "Let's do it!"

1. Are Jesse, Maurice, Consuela, and Max working as a team? Explain.

_____

_____

2. Which worker shows the best leadership skills? Why do you think so?

_____

_____

3. Do you think Maurice's negative comments should cause him to be replaced by another production worker? Why or why not?

_____

_____

4. Which worker took the initiative to get everyone on task?

_____

_____

5. Are Jesse, Maurice, Consuela, and Max sharing responsibility for reaching an outcome? Explain.

_____

_____

6. How well do you think the four co-workers will work as a team? Why?

_____

_____

7. What should the team do if management does not OK all its ideas?

_____

_____

WRITE IT

Imagine that you are part of a team and need to bring ideas to a discussion about fire and safety issues. Think about fire and safety issues in your workplace, school, or home. On a separate sheet of paper, write a list of ideas for improving safety conditions. You may want to refer to the "Problem solving with a team" section of the "Problem-Solving Checklists" on page 188.

Being Part of an Effective Team

In the video, what qualities and skills made workers effective team members? When asked, did workers offer suggestions that showed they were willing to take responsibility for solutions?

Leadership Skills	Interpersonal, Problem-Solving Skills
• Take initiative and responsibility. • Make suggestions. • Be willing to follow a plan or directions. • Work to capacity. • Follow through. • Openly express your thoughts and beliefs. • Respect others.	• Identify the needs of the team. • Cooperate and help others on the team. • Appreciate the **diversity** of the team. • Encourage and **motivate** others. • Explore solutions with team members. • Use strategies that strengthen the team. • Put team needs above personal needs.

1. Which leadership skills do you need to develop?

_____

2. Which interpersonal and problem-solving skills do you need to develop?

_____

Balancing the Individual with the Whole to Meet Goals

Being part of an effective team is a balancing act. Team members must continually balance the needs of individuals with the needs of the team. Appreciate differences in personalities, backgrounds, experiences, and outlooks. Play off each other's strengths and make up for each other's weaknesses. Also remember that everyone has private issues, such as personal and family concerns; concerns about salary, bonuses, and other work incentives; or concerns about job satisfaction and advancement. Share concerns like these only when they affect your work — as, for example, when you need to take time off. Don't pry when others have problems; offer to help. In this way, your team will build trust and a sense of security.

Write *Yes* if the issue is appropriate for a work team to discuss; *No* if it is not appropriate.

_____ 1. Scheduling problems

_____ 2. A team member's salary

_____ 3. A team member's absences

_____ 4. A team member's divorce

_____ 5. Ways to help each other

_____ 6. Constructive ways to criticize each other's work

Organizing to Function as a Successful Team

How does a team continue to work successfully? Being organized is a must! A team leader may be either appointed, selected by the group, or self-nominated. The leader should be someone who can guide discussions and decisions, help the team identify and carry out its plan, and help communicate with people outside the team. Having a team leader, however, does not mean other members do not use their leadership qualities. All team members need leadership skills to work together and to form and carry out the team's specific plan.

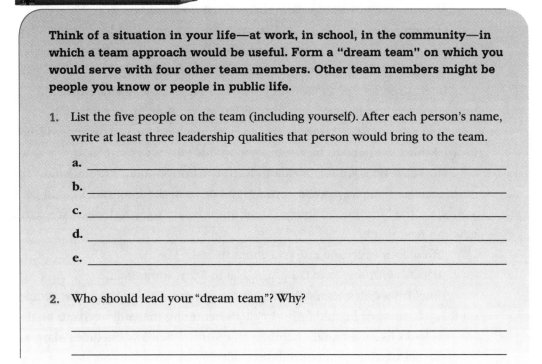

Think of a situation in your life—at work, in school, in the community—in which a team approach would be useful. Form a "dream team" on which you would serve with four other team members. Other team members might be people you know or people in public life.

1. List the five people on the team (including yourself). After each person's name, write at least three leadership qualities that person would bring to the team.

   a. _____

   b. _____

   c. _____

   d. _____

   e. _____

2. Who should lead your "dream team"? Why?

   _____

   _____

MANUFACTURING: Mayela is the leader of a sewing team for a clothing manufacturer. It is her job to motivate her co-workers, establish procedures, be sure the sewers change machines for different tasks, and suggest the order of work. She has called a meeting with the sewing team to discuss details for a new job the team will be starting next week.

Communication Strategies

Read the conversation below. Then answer the questions that follow.

"OK, everybody. Listen up," calls Mayela. "Next week we're starting a new job making women's blouses. As usual, we'll be paid by the number of quality pieces we make. With this job, though, we'll also get a bonus if we meet our goal. So let's get organized."

"Will we be working our usual places on the assembly line for blouses?" asks Irma.

"I don't see why not," says Mayela. "What do all of you think?"

"I agree," says Jay. "We're familiar with our machines, and we know which parts of the blouses need to be sewn before the others. I think we should keep the procedure the same so we can meet our deadline."

Imelda speaks up, "Is there any way I could learn to operate the buttonholer? I was hoping to work a different machine on our next job."

"I'm not sure. The buttonholer is a new machine for you, which will slow us up. I think we need to meet our goal on this job," says Mayela.

"It would be good for Imelda to learn the buttonholer," argues Irma. "The more machines she learns, the better for all of us in the long run. I could get her started on the buttonholer today. I think she'd be up to speed when we start the new job next week."

"How does everyone else feel about it?" asks Mayela.

"It's OK with me," says Lucy. "She has to learn sometime."

"Imelda's a quick learner," adds Jay. "And we're a little ahead of schedule on this job, anyway. I could finish Imelda's hemming that still needs to be done."

"It looks like everyone's behind you on this, Imelda," concludes Mayela. "You can start training on buttonholes today."

Match the leadership and interpersonal problem-solving skills to the appropriate team members. Some skills will be used more than once.

Team Members

_____ 1. Mayela

_____ 2. Irma

_____ 3. Lucy

_____ 4. Imelda

_____ 5. Jay

Skills

a. Takes initiative

b. Shows responsibility

c. Makes suggestions

d. Is willing to follow a plan

e. Listens and respects others

f. Explores solutions

g. Guides the discussion

6. In what ways did the team balance Imelda's individual needs with the whole team's needs?

_____

_____

7. Rate the sewing team on a scale of 1 to 5, with 5 being the most effective. Consider the personal and interpersonal problem-solving skills of each team member. Also consider the leadership and cooperative qualities of the team. Explain your rating.

_____

_____

_____

MATH MATTERS ....

In addition to individual team members' hourly wages, the team as a whole will earn $0.60 for each completed blouse. If the team makes 325 blouses in one week, how much will each team member earn in bonuses for the week? Explain how you got your answer.

_____

_____

Review

Reading about effective communication is only the first step toward becoming a better communicator. The next steps are to:

STEP 1: Apply the skills described.
STEP 2: Evaluate how well you did.
STEP 3: Make a personal action plan.

During the review that follows, you will take all three of these steps.

STEP 1: Apply Your Skills

The best place to apply effective team communication skills in the workplace is, of course, at work. Think of a work team you will communicate with in the next few days, such as a team that has been organized to solve a problem or meet a goal. If you don't have a job right now, think of a personal situation in which you will use teamwork skills.

On the lines below, describe the team you selected.

1. What team do you plan to communicate with?

    _____

2. When will you communicate with this team?

    _____

3. What is the purpose of the team?

    _____

4. What would you like the outcome of the team's efforts to be?

    _____

During the communication with the team, you will practice:
*   Approaching the task as a team player.
*   Sharing responsibility for the outcome of the team's efforts.
*   Showing leadership qualities as an effective team member.

Review the skills you should apply. Read the Listening and Speaking Checklists on page 190 and the Problem-Solving Checklists on page 188-189.

STEP 2: Self-Evaluation (right after the communication)

Evaluate how well you applied the teamwork communication skills. Complete the following questionnaire as soon after the communication as possible.

1. During the communication, I . . .

   Yes No

   ☐ ☐ **a.** Asked questions to understand the team's task.

   ☐ ☐ **b.** Helped to identify what would make the team successful.

   ☐ ☐ **c.** Worked together to develop one or more plans of action.

   ☐ ☐ **d.** Helped the team to consider the pros and cons of a plan.

   ☐ ☐ **e.** Respected differences in teammates' personalities, backgrounds, experiences, and outlooks.

   ☐ ☐ **f.** Gave ideas, information, and help in meeting a goal.

   ☐ ☐ **g.** Spoke up if there was a problem and suggested solutions.

   ☐ ☐ **h.** Offered encouragement to teammates.

   ☐ ☐ **i.** Showed leadership and problem-solving skills.

   ☐ ☐ **j.** Helped to communicate the plan and put it into effect.

   ☐ ☐ **k.** Helped to evaluate the outcome and make changes.

2. Was the team successful? In other words, was the outcome what you hoped it would be? Explain why or why not.

   _____

3. Which skills do you think you applied particularly well?

   _____

4. Which skills would you like to practice further? Why?

   _____

STEP 3: Personal Action Plan (over the next two weeks)

An action plan is a series of steps you take to reach a goal. In this case, your goal is to see what you learned from the self-evaluation, plan to be a good team member, and evaluate your progress over the next two weeks.

Answer these questions to make your plan and assess your progress.

1. **Which communication skills do you most need to develop?** Review the self-evaluation you completed on page 69, and choose two or three skills that you answered *No* to. If necessary, talk your choices over with a supervisor or friend. Or complete the self-evaluation again, only this time imagine how the other person would evaluate you. Be honest!

   I need to develop the following communication skills:

   _____

2. **Over what period will you work at improving these skills?** (Choose ten days in the near future.)

   I will work to improve these skills from _____ to _____.

3. **What will you do to develop the skills you choose?** Be specific. Review this unit and the checklists on pages 188–190; then write down what you plan to do in future teamwork communications.

   In my teamwork communications, I will

   _____

4. **How will you measure your progress?** One way is to use the questionnaire on page 69 to evaluate the teamwork communications you have each day. Another way is to discuss your plan with a team member and ask the person to help you evaluate your progress. A third way is to keep a "teamwork communication journal" by noting what did and did not go well each day.

   I will keep track of my progress by

   _____

5. **How will you evaluate what you learned during the two weeks?** As a final step, evaluate what you learned. Ask yourself, "What am I doing now that I didn't do before? What are the positive effects of my efforts?"

   By following the action plan, I learned to

   _____

Communicating with Customers

The video program you are about to watch will help you see why good customer service is essential to business success. You will see how **customer service representatives** work to meet the needs of customers and the business, and you will learn ways to work with difficult customers.

While you watch the video, imagine that you are the customer. Think about how you would feel if you were the one upset with a company's service or product. Ask yourself what you would want the business to do to solve the problem.

Remember that conflict resolution techniques can be applied to all areas of life. At work and at home, you can settle misunderstandings by being calm, listening, finding out why the other person is upset, and working out a solution everyone can agree with.

OBJECTIVE

In this lesson, you will work with the following concepts and skills:

1. **Understanding how satisfied customers benefit you and your business**
2. **Learning ways to meet customers' needs**
3. **Solving problems with difficult customers**

Sneak Preview

This exercise previews some of the concepts from Program 12. After you answer the questions, use the Feedback on page 73 to help set your learning goals.

SERVICE: As a postal clerk, Joe must sell stamps, weigh packages, and process mail-forwarding orders. It's been a busy day, and customers have long waits in line. An elderly woman steps up to Joe's counter.

"Good afternoon, ma'am," Joe says with more cheer than he feels.

"Yes," she replies absently, handing a mail-forwarding card to Joe. "I want to have my mail forwarded to Florida, starting November 3."

Joe notes that the customer seems tired and grumpy. Thinking that she could use a good laugh, he says, "Well, that's fine. But I need proof of birth of your mother, your husband, and all your children!"

Confused, the woman asks, "What did you say?"

Joe repeats himself, smiling widely so that she knows he's kidding. But the woman doesn't see the humor and appears quite shaken.

"I don't understand," she says in a quivering voice. "I've never had to give this information before. Look at how old I am," she waves her arms from head to toes. "Do you think my mother could possibly be *alive?* You want to know about my children? They've all grown up and moved away. As for my husband, he passed away just two months ago. Listen, can't you just forward my mail to Florida as usual?"

Joe looks at the woman. Her eyes are filling with tears. He feels embarrassed and wishes he had not mistaken her loneliness for a bad mood. "I'm so sorry," Joe says sincerely. "I was only joking, trying to make you smile. Of course we can forward your mail." Joe reads her name and the information she has provided on the card. "We'll start forwarding your mail on the third. When you return, just let us know, and we'll deliver your mail to your home here as usual." Joe looks the customer in the eye and says, "I apologize for upsetting you, Mrs. Jablonski. I hope your stay in Florida is a good one."

Mrs. Jablonski nods her head once and gives a slight wave of her hand as she walks away. Joe still feels bad.

Write *Yes* if Joe displayed a customer service skill; *No* if he did not.

_____ 1. Provided timely service

_____ 2. Presented a positive personal image

_____ 3. Identified what the customer wanted

_____ 4. Understood how the customer felt about the situation

_____ 5. Determined what would satisfy the customer

_____ 6. Identified the reasons why the customer was upset

_____ 7. Stayed calm

_____ 8. Avoided frustrating the customer

Feedback for Sneak Preview

- If you got all of the answers right . . .   you have a basic understanding of how to communicate with customers. While watching the video, focus on the correct way to meet customers' needs.

- If you missed question 1 or 2 . . .   you need a better understanding of the importance of customer satisfaction.

- If you missed question 3, 4, or 5 . . .   you need to learn how to provide for customers' needs.

- If you missed question 6, 7, or 8 . . .   you need to learn how to work with difficult customers.

Vocabulary for *Communicating with Customers*

competition	businesses that offer similar products or services to a similar customer base
customer base	a business's current and potential customers
customer satisfaction	the degree to which customers' expectations are met
customer service representatives	employees who specialize in taking customers' orders, providing product or service information, and handling customer complaints
repeat customers	customers who go to the same business again and again
subcontractor	an independent worker or business hired by another business to do a specific job

Now watch Program 12.

After you watch, work on:
- pages 75–190 in this workbook
- Internet activities at www.pbs.org/literacy

AFTER you WATCH

program **12**

Communicating with Customers

On the following pages, you will learn more about the issues discussed in the video program and have an opportunity to develop your skills.

Think About the Key Points from the Video Program

As an employee, you must understand the importance of **customer satisfaction** and show that you understand by:

- Providing good customer service.
- Recognizing the benefits of customer satisfaction.
- Trying to build your business's **customer base.**

To provide for customers' needs, you must:

- Identify what the customer wants.
- Understand how a customer feels about a situation.
- Determine what will satisfy the customer.

When working with difficult customers, you should:

- Find out why the customer is upset.
- Apply the do's and don'ts of customer service.
- Use the language of problem solving.

Understanding the Importance of Customer Satisfaction

As you saw in the video program, customer service is every employee's business, regardless of his or her job. Why is customer satisfaction so important? Every business has **competition.** No matter what business you work for, other businesses offer similar products and services at similar prices. To stand out, your business must provide excellent service. Good service helps build a strong customer base, because satisfied customers return again. They also spread the word about your business to their family and friends. With a strong customer base of **repeat customers** and new ones brought in by positive word of mouth, businesses are able to succeed.

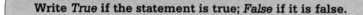

Write *True* if the statement is true; *False* if it is false.

_____ 1. A business can distinguish itself from competitors by providing good service.

_____ 2. Customers always care more about price than service.

_____ 3. Word of mouth can help a business succeed.

_____ 4. Employees who don't work with customers needn't be concerned about customer service.

Providing Customer Service

If you answer customers' questions, refer customers to the appropriate person or department, listen to customers' complaints, or help solve customers' problems, then you need to be concerned with customer satisfaction. In fact, you need to be concerned regardless of what you do, because if your business does not satisfy its customers, it will not survive. Remember that when a customer walks into your place of business, you may be one of the first people he or she sees. What kind of first impression do you make? Do you represent your business— and yourself—in a positive light? Follow the three steps below.

Three Steps to a Positive Personal Image

1. **Good Grooming:** Make sure that your clothes, hairstyle, and overall grooming reflect the image of the company.

2. **Positive Body Language:** Send a positive message with your facial expressions, gestures, and other body language.

3. **Appropriate Tone of Voice:** Use a calm and steady tone of voice.

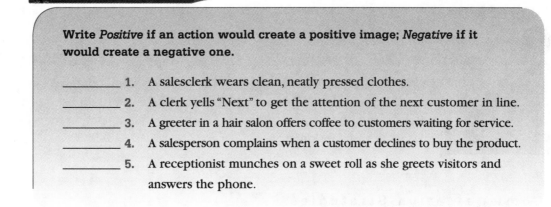

Write *Positive* if an action would create a positive image; *Negative* if it would create a negative one.

_____ 1. A salesclerk wears clean, neatly pressed clothes.

_____ 2. A clerk yells "Next" to get the attention of the next customer in line.

_____ 3. A greeter in a hair salon offers coffee to customers waiting for service.

_____ 4. A salesperson complains when a customer declines to buy the product.

_____ 5. A receptionist munches on a sweet roll as she greets visitors and answers the phone.

Understanding How Customer Satisfaction Benefits You

Customer satisfaction benefits more than your business. It benefits you, too. You've probably noticed that when your customers are satisfied, your job is a lot easier and less stressful. Developing good "people skills" is also a wise business move, because skills in customer service will help you find and keep a good job. You can be sure that employees who work well with the public will always be in demand. The fact is, when you help your customers, you are also helping yourself.

Think of a time when you answered customers' questions; referred customers to other departments, companies, or clients; listened to customers' complaints; or resolved customers' problems. Briefly describe how you provided good customer service and how you felt.

If you have never worked directly with customers, describe a time when you as a customer benefited from good customer service.

_____

_____

_____

_____

_____

SERVICE: Part of your job as general manager of Abracadabra Pest Control Company is to monitor customer satisfaction. Three months before a customer's contract is to expire, you send the customer a customer satisfaction survey.

Communication Strategies

On this page and the next, read the survey that was completed by the Heritage Condominium Association, one of Abracadabra's customers. Use what you have learned about providing customer satisfaction to determine the best way to respond to the survey.

Your Pests Magically Disappear
ABRACADABRA PEST CONTROL
customer survey

1. Was the Abracadabra service technician friendly?
Yes ☑   No ☐

2. Was the service technician able to answer your questions?
Always ☐   Sometimes ☑   Never ☐

3. What image did the service technician present?
Very professional ☐   Somewhat professional ☑   Not professional at all ☐

4. Were pest management materials applied safely and neatly?
Yes ☑   No ☐

5. Did the service technician say thank you before leaving?
Yes ☑   No ☐

6. Overall, how satisfied were you with the service technician?

Very satisfied ☐   Somewhat satisfied ☐

Somewhat dissatisfied ☑   Very dissatisfied ☐

7. Were our pest management materials effective?

Yes ☑   No ☐

8. Would you recommend Abracadabra Pest Control to a friend?

Yes ☐   No ☑

9. Do you have specific complaints about the service you received from Abracadabra Pest Control?

When we signed our contract, we gave you a key to the basement so the technician could service

it each month. He did not service the basement unless I walked him through. He was nice, but he

didn't work independently and couldn't answer questions about pest control methods.

---

1. What seems to be the cause of the customer's dissatisfaction?

    (1) The pest management materials made people in the building sick.
    (2) Abracadabra lost the keys to the basement.
    (3) The technician did not meet the customer's service expectations.
    (4) The pest management materials were ineffective.

2. Which course of action is most likely to satisfy the customer?

    (1) Look at the survey when the contract is to be renewed.
    (2) Retrain the technician in effective pest control methods.
    (3) Send the customer a brochure that explains pest control methods.
    (4) Call the customer, apologize, and discuss how you can provide better service.

3. What should the technician do on his next service call to this customer?

    (1) Look sorry and promise to do better in the future.
    (2) Apologize for mistakes and follow the customer's instructions.
    (3) Smile and offer to give the customer a lesson in pest control.
    (4) Act as if nothing happened and go about his business.

READ IT

Ask a business such as a bank or a large grocery store for a booklet that explains its services.
On a separate piece of paper, explain how the business tries to provide good customer service.

Providing for Customers' Needs

To provide for customers' needs, you must understand what they are. That's why customer service representatives begin by identifying what their customers need. Representatives talk with customers and ask questions to better understand these needs. They also "read" their customers' facial expressions and tones of voice. By speaking and listening to their customers, service representatives find out what they need to know. Some customers have problems they want solved. Some want the service representatives to understand their complaints, requests, or comments. Others want to feel that their business is important to the service representatives and to the company.

Describe what the customer wants in each situation below. Write *PS* if a problem needs to be solved; *U* if a complaint, request, or suggestion needs to be understood; or *I* if the customer wants to feel that his or her business is important.

_____ 1. "Do you realize how costly your mistake may be to my business?"

_____ 2. "I've been a customer for many years, but that doesn't seem to matter to you."

_____ 3. "I ordered a pizza an hour and a half ago, but it still isn't here."

_____ 4. "Will you leave the package at the back door if I leave a note with my signature, address, and date on it?"

_____ 5. "I was told that my photographs would be here at the store by 4:30 today. It's 6:00, so where are my photos?"

Identifying Problem Situations

When someone you know has a problem, you can sense it by the person's tone of voice, facial expressions, and body language. Watch for those same signals in your customers to identify when they are upset. Try to identify feelings such as satisfaction, frustration, patience, impatience, and anger. After you tune in to a customer's feelings, ask questions to find out what the customer thinks caused the problem. Typical concerns are complaints about the quality of a service or product, lack of skill or interest on the part of an employee, and understandable mistakes. Once you identify the cause of a problem, you are well on your way to finding a solution.

Think about the signals you send when you experience different emotions. Describe the tone of voice, facial expression, and body language you use for each feeling listed in the chart below.

Feeling	Tone of voice	Facial expression	Body language
Satisfaction			
Frustration			
Patience			
Impatience			
Anger			

Ensuring Customer Satisfaction

After you identify a customer's needs and the causes of a problem, the next step is to find ways to solve the problem. One of the best ways to find out what a customer wants is simply to ask. The customer may need only an answer, a reasonable explanation, or a suggestion. Or the customer may want a specific product or service, a timely replacement, or credit. If you can't give the customer what he or she wants, courteously explain why and offer an alternative.

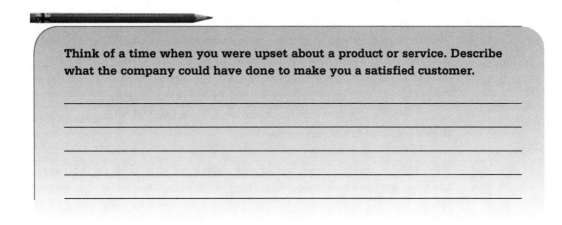

Think of a time when you were upset about a product or service. Describe what the company could have done to make you a satisfied customer.

_____

_____

_____

_____

CONSTRUCTION: Eric is a **subcontractor** who installs vinyl flooring for National Floor Coverings. He recently installed new kitchen flooring for Mrs. Bell. After Eric finished the job and left, Mrs. Bell noticed that the job was not done well. Her neighbor agreed. Mrs. Bell wrote a letter to National Floor Coverings.

Communication Strategies

Read the letter and answer the questions that follow.

felicia bell

582 Buena Vista Avenue
San Diego, CA 92109
\<Date\>

National Floor Coverings
2340 5th Avenue
San Diego, CA 92103

Dear Sir or Madam:

I'm writing to tell you how dissatisfied I am with the installation of the new vinyl flooring in my kitchen. A week ago Eric, the installer whom you subcontracted my job to, came to my house to lay down the flooring that I had ordered. Eric was a very nice man, and he was very neat. But his skill at installing vinyl floors was not as good. The vinyl flooring doesn't touch the walls on two sides of the kitchen. There's also a dent in the middle of the floor where Eric dropped his toolbox. And part of the valve to the gas line broke off when Eric shoved the stove back into place.

A week has passed since the floor was installed, and I've already paid my bill in full. But I want you to know how disappointed I am with your company. I had heard good things about National Floor Coverings, but I have to wonder about a company that subcontracts a quality product such as yours to an unskilled installer.

Sincerely,

Felicia Bell

Felicia Bell

1. According to the letter, what does Mrs. Bell want?

   (1) to have the flooring replaced
   (2) to get a refund
   (3) to inform the manager about the bad installation job
   (4) to complain about the subcontractor's rudeness

2. How does Mrs. Bell feel about the situation?

   (1) disappointed
   (2) furious
   (3) apologetic
   (4) satisfied

3. What does Mrs. Bell think caused the situation?

   (1) an uneven kitchen floor
   (2) an unskilled installer
   (3) a gas line problem
   (4) a bad product

4. What is the best way for the manager to find out what will satisfy Mrs. Bell?

   (1) telephone Mrs. Bell
   (2) send Mrs. Bell a letter
   (3) talk to Eric
   (4) recall what other customers have wanted in the past

5. Briefly describe what you would do to make Mrs. Bell a satisfied customer.

   _____

   _____

   _____

   _____

   _____

MATH MATTERS

One of the manager's solutions was to give Mrs. Bell a 20% refund on her bill. Mrs. Bell paid $688.72 for the vinyl flooring. Another solution was to give a 15% discount on Mrs. Bell's next purchase at National Flooring Company. She has priced new carpeting, padding, and installation for her living room at $1,094.40. Which solution gives Mrs. Bell the greater savings? By how much?

Working with Difficult Customers

Let's face it. Every one of us has been a difficult customer at some time. And chances are the employees dealing with our disagreeable selves didn't cause the problem. How do employees remain calm when customers aren't? They remind themselves to find the reason why the customer is being difficult. They understand that frustration with a defective product, a clerk's lack of interest or skill, or past unpleasant experiences with customer service representatives can make even the most patient person angry. They also understand that people sometimes have a bad day and take it out on others. Whatever the problem, the customer service representative stays calm by approaching the situation as if the situation, not the person, is difficult.

1. Think of a time when you were a difficult customer. How did the employee handle the situation?

   _____

   _____

2. Did the employee handle the situation well? Explain why or why not.

   _____

Developing Strategies for Dealing with Customer Complaints

As an employee dealing with customer complaints, you might want to keep in mind these basic service strategies.

Service Strategies	
Do's	*Don'ts*
• *Do* make repeat business your goal. • *Do* stay and sound calm. • *Do* find a solution. • *Do* follow through. • *Do* refer the customer to someone else when necessary.	• *Don't* take it personally. • *Don't* get baited. • *Don't* blame the customer. • *Don't* make false promises. • *Don't* just pass the customer along to someone else.

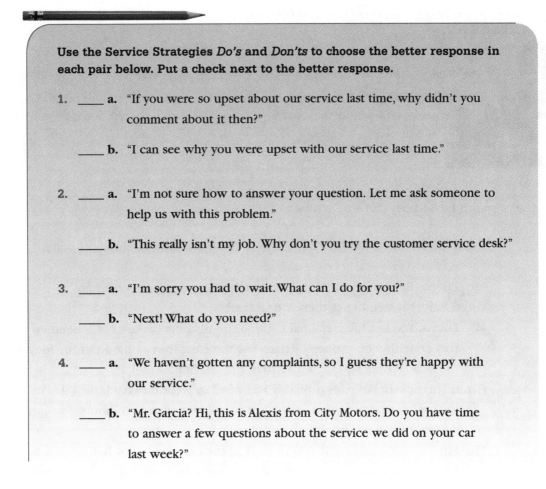

Use the Service Strategies *Do's* and *Don'ts* to choose the better response in each pair below. Put a check next to the better response.

1. ____ **a.** "If you were so upset about our service last time, why didn't you comment about it then?"

   ____ **b.** "I can see why you were upset with our service last time."

2. ____ **a.** "I'm not sure how to answer your question. Let me ask someone to help us with this problem."

   ____ **b.** "This really isn't my job. Why don't you try the customer service desk?"

3. ____ **a.** "I'm sorry you had to wait. What can I do for you?"

   ____ **b.** "Next! What do you need?"

4. ____ **a.** "We haven't gotten any complaints, so I guess they're happy with our service."

   ____ **b.** "Mr. Garcia? Hi, this is Alexis from City Motors. Do you have time to answer a few questions about the service we did on your car last week?"

Using Problem-Solving Language

When working with difficult customers, begin by calming them down. Keep a friendly tone of voice, look the customer in the eyes, and assure him or her that you want to help. Once the customer is calm, you can more easily identify the problem and the customer's needs. Also use problem-solving language, such as clearly explaining what you are going to do to help. Maintain a positive attitude by telling the customer what you *can* do rather than what you *can't* do. If the customer doesn't agree with your solution, ask him or her to help you find an alternate solution. If the customer is still dissatisfied, ask a supervisor for help. Above all, avoid frustrating the customer further.

Think of a time in your personal life or at work when you were faced with a difficult person. How did you calm the person?

_____

_____

SERVICE: Gina is an auto mechanic for King Brakes. She installed new brakes on Mr. Turro's car yesterday. He has brought the car back with a complaint.

Communication Strategies

Read the situation below. Then answer the questions on the next page.

Mr. Turro: Remember me? You put new brakes on my car yesterday.

Gina: Sure, I remember. Is there a problem?

Mr. Turro: You bet there is. I paid you in full for new brakes, but I assumed you had done the job properly. That's not the case. Every time I put my foot on the brakes, they squeak worse than the old brakes did!

Gina: The new brake pads probably just need to wear down a little. I'll take a look at them if you want me to, but it will be a couple of hours. I've got several cars ahead of yours now.

Mr. Turro: Wait a minute. It seems like I'm the one losing out here. The way I see it, you have been paid in full for a job that's not finished. The least you can do is put my car next in line.

Gina: Sorry, but these customers were here first. You'll have to wait, unless you want to bring the car back sometime when we're not busy.

Mr. Turro: And when would that be?

Gina: Well, if you could bring it in first thing in the morning on a Tuesday or Wednesday, I could probably look at it.

Mr. Turro: I'll do that if you'll give me an appointment so I'm not waiting all day again.

Gina: Sorry, but we don't take appointments. You'll just have to take a chance that we won't be busy.

Mr. Turro: This is incredible! Do you treat all your customers this way? Or is this special treatment reserved for those of us who pay our bills in full?

Gina: Hey, I don't have to take this from you. If you want me to look at your car, either sit down and wait or come back later. It's up to you.

Mr. Turro: Fine. I'll wait now—and only because you already have my money for this job. You'd better do the job right this time!

Use what you have learned about dealing with difficult customers to answer these questions.

1. Why was Mr. Turro upset when he first came in?

   _____

2. What added to Mr. Turro's frustration?

   _____

3. What Service Strategies *Do's* and *Don'ts* did Gina fail to follow?

   _____

   _____

   _____

   _____

   _____

   _____

4. What problem-solving language should Gina have used?

   _____

   _____

   _____

5. How could Gina have balanced Mr. Turro's needs with those of her other customers? Write one possible solution and one alternate solution.

   _____

   _____

   _____

   _____

WRITE IT •

Imagine that you are Gina's boss and that you overheard her conversation with Mr. Turro. How would you handle the situation? What would you do to satisfy Mr. Turro? On a separate sheet of paper, explain what you would do.

Review

Reading about effective communication is only the first step toward becoming a better communicator. The next steps are to:

STEP 1: Apply the skills described.
STEP 2: Evaluate how well the skills were applied.
STEP 3: Make a personal action plan.

During the review that follows, you will take all three of these steps.

STEP 1: Apply Your Skills

The best place to apply effective communication skills with customers is, of course, at work. Think of a time you had to work out a problem for a customer who was angry or upset. If you've never worked with customers, think of a time when you, as a customer, were upset with a business.

On the lines below, describe the conversation you selected.

1. When and where did the conversation take place?

   _____

   _____

2. What was the situation? Why was the customer upset? (If you were the customer, explain why you were upset.)

   _____

   _____

3. What was the outcome of the conversation?

   _____

   _____

   _____

Read the Listening and Speaking Checklists on page 190 and the Problem-Solving Checklists on page 188–189 to review the skills you or the employee you dealt with should have applied.

STEP 2: Evaluation

Evaluate how well you or the salesclerk communicated. Complete the following questionnaire as soon after the conversation as possible.

Yes No

- ☐ ☐ **1.** I (or the employee) used an appropriate tone of voice.
- ☐ ☐ **2.** I (or the employee) stayed and sounded calm.
- ☐ ☐ **3.** I identified the customer's needs (or the employee identified mine).
- ☐ ☐ **4.** I correctly interpreted the customer's nonverbal clues (or the employee correctly interpreted mine).
- ☐ ☐ **5.** I (or the employee) asked questions to find out the cause of the problem.
- ☐ ☐ **6.** I tried to understand the customer's feelings (or the employee tried to understand mine).
- ☐ ☐ **7.** I asked the customer what would satisfy her or him (or the employee asked questions to see what would satisfy me).
- ☐ ☐ **8.** I explained what could be done to resolve the problem (or the employee explained a solution to me).
- ☐ ☐ **9.** I followed through to be sure the customer was satisfied (or the employee followed through to be sure I was satisfied).

10. Was the conversation successful? In other words, were you able to solve the problem to the customer's satisfaction? (If you were the customer, were you satisfied with the way the problem was handled?) Explain why or why not.

_____

_____

_____

STEP 3: Personal Action Plan

An action plan is a series of steps you take to reach a goal. In this case, your goal is to take what you learned from the evaluation and plan how to be a better communicator.

Answer these questions to make your plan.

1. **Which communication skills would you like to work on?** Review the evaluation you completed on page 89, and choose two or three skills that you answered *No* to. (If you were the customer, analyze what you learned from the situation. What communication skills listed would you most like to have when working with customers?)

   I would like to develop the following communication skills:

   _____

2. **What will you do to develop the skills you choose?** Review this unit and the checklists on pages 188–190; then write down what you plan to do in future conversations with people who are angry or upset.

   In my conversations over the next two weeks, I will:

   _____

   _____

3. **How will you measure your progress?** One way is to use the questionnaire on page 89 to evaluate the conversations you have each day. Another way is to discuss the plan with a co-worker or family member and ask the person to help you evaluate your progress. A third way is to keep a "communication journal" and note what communications did and did not go well each day.

   I will keep track of my progress by

   _____

4. **How will you evaluate what you learned during the two weeks?** As a final step, evaluate what you learned. Ask yourself, "What am I doing now that I didn't do before? What are the positive effects of my efforts?"

   By following the action plan, I learned to

   _____

BEFORE you WATCH

program **13**

A Process
for Writing

In the video program you are about to watch, you will learn why writing is an important communication tool in the workplace. You will also be presented with some basic steps that you can follow to write well on the job. These steps are called the writing process.

While you watch the video, notice the types of writing done at work. Find out how business writing differs from other types of writing. And notice the type of language and usage that are appropriate at work.

Compare what you learn about business writing to the types of writing you do in your everyday life. How is a note you write to a spouse or child similar to writing a note to a co-worker? How is writing a letter to a friend similar to writing a letter to a customer? How is making a grocery list similar to writing a list of things to do on the job? When you compare business writing to the writing you already do, you may discover that you already know some of the basics of workplace writing!

Sneak Preview

This exercise previews some of the concepts from Program 13. After you answer the questions, use the Feedback on page 93 to help set your learning goals.

MANUFACTURING: Jan Lemberg, a sales representative for Reliable Tool & Die Wholesalers, received a voice mail order on her telephone. Jan responded to her customer as follows.

RELIABLE TOOL & DIE WHOLESALERS

Opus Industrial Park
Kankakee, IL 60901
Telephone 815-444-9977 • Fax 815-444-9978

FAX MEMO_____ **Date:** November 5, 1999

TO—
Contact name: Craig Robinson, Purchasing Agent
Company name: HOME HARDWARE, INC.

FROM—
Sender: Jan Lemberg, Sales Representative
Description: Thank you for your telephone order of November 4, 1998.
All the items are in stock in our warehouse, so I went ahead and processed your order. Here is confirmation of that order for your records. We have charged your account #83075 as requested.

Item	Part Number	Unit Price	Total
25 hammers	B-432-S	@$5.50	$137.50
15 chisels	RS-510S	4.75	71.25
30 measuring tapes	D-43988	8.50	255.00
30 screw drivers	S-207-23P	6.00	180.00
TOTAL			$643.75

You can expect delivery of the complete order on or about November 11. Be sure to call me if you have any problems with delivery or with the shipment when received.

Jan Lemberg

Evaluate Jan's message. Write *True* if a statement about the message is true; *False* if it is false.

_____ 1. The purpose of Jan's message is to point out and correct an error in an order.

_____ 2. The message is formatted as a memo and was sent by fax.

_____ 3. The message is poorly organized.

_____ 4. The message is confusing and difficult to read.

_____ 5. The message explains what Jan did and what the customer should do.

_____ 6. The message contains grammatical and spelling errors.

Feedback

- If you got all of the answers right . . .   you have a basic understanding of written workplace communications. While watching the video, focus on the process of writing.

- If you missed question 1, 2, or 3 . . .   you need practice in recognizing effective business writing.

- If you missed question 4 or 5 . . .   you need to become more familiar with workplace writing.

- If you missed question 6 . . .   you need to learn more about the appropriate language to use in business writing.

Vocabulary for *A Process for Writing*

audience	recipients; readers; people who are to receive a message
e-mail	messages that are keyed into a computer and sent electronically
faxes	written messages that are copied on a fax machine and sent using telephone signals
forms	standardized messages with blank lines for filling in information
formal language	words and phrases used in formal situations, such as business transactions
format	the form in which a message is organized, written, and set up on one or more pages
inventory	a complete and detailed list of items, often with their estimated value
jargon	business or technical language that is difficult for people unfamiliar with a business to understand
memos	brief written business messages that begin with the standard headings *To, From, Date, Subject*
proofread	to read a message carefully to find and correct errors
revise	to rewrite a message to improve it
slang	very informal words and expressions used in informal situations among friends
"you" attitude	an approach to writing in which the reader is given the benefits of taking an action

PBS LiteracyLink®

Now watch Program 13.

After you watch, work on:
- pages 95–110 in this workbook
- Internet activities at www.pbs.org/literacy

AFTER you WATCH

program **13**

A Process for Writing

On the following pages, you will learn more about the issues discussed in the video program and have an opportunity to develop your skills.

Think About the Key Points from the Video Program

To be an effective business writer, you must:
- Understand the purposes of workplace writing.
- Produce accurate and well-organized messages.
- Follow a process when you write.

To show that you understand how to write for the workplace, you should:
- Present facts rather than personal opinions.
- Focus on the receiver's needs as you write.
- Produce professional-looking messages.

To show that you know the language of business, you should:
- Avoid using **slang.**
- Write clearly and to the point.
- Use correct grammar, punctuation, capitalization, and spelling.

Becoming an Effective Writer

As you saw in the video program, all employees write on the job. You write to apply for a job, complete time cards, or fill out insurance forms. You write notes to your supervisor to ask for a day off, report problems with equipment, or set up a time to meet. You write when you take **inventory,** ship packages, list instructions, and send **e-mails.** In short, you write to:

- Ask and answer questions.
- Inform others about actions you have taken or problems that have arisen.
- Persuade others to take action.

Think of a business message you recently received at work or at home.

1. Who wrote to you?

   _____

2. What was the purpose of the message?

   _____

3. Was the message a note? Memo? Letter? Form? Why was this **format** used?

   _____

4. Was the message hand-delivered, mailed, faxed, or e-mailed? Why did the sender use this method of delivery?

   _____

Writing Is Critical to Business Success

Imagine a workplace in which no one ever wrote. Employees would line up to tell supervisors about problems, customer orders, schedules, vacations, and injuries. Everyone would have to rely on memory to recall instructions and fill orders. Workers on day shifts would stay late to give progress reports to the night shift. Customers and businesses would argue about what was ordered, how much it cost, and whether the order was correct.

Writing creates a record of what was requested, said, and done. Writing can also be a convenient way to communicate with co-workers, supervisors, and customers. To provide those benefits, business writing must be accurate, well organized, and easy to read.

You are e-mailing a supplier to explain that an order is missing several items. What information do you need to include in your message? Place a check next to all that apply.

_____ **a.** the date of the order

_____ **b.** the date you started working

_____ **c.** the item numbers and names of the missing items

_____ **d.** the name of the person who uses the items

_____ **e.** the quantity ordered and the quantity received

Adapting the Writing Process to Fit Your Needs

To produce effective messages, business writers follow a process. The chart below describes each step to take. These steps can be adapted to fit any type of writing. For example, if you're writing a memo, you should follow all the steps. But if you're filling out a form, you can skip steps 3 and 5.

The Writing Process

1. Identify your purpose, or reason for writing, and audience.

2. Gather facts and organize your thoughts.

3. Select an appropriate format, such as a letter, memo, report, or list.

4. Write a first draft.

5. Review and **revise** your first draft, alone or with a co-worker.

6. **Proofread** your final draft for errors, alone or with a co-worker.

7. Distribute your writing by delivering or sending it.

Each thought below goes with a step in the writing process. Write the number of the step on the line.

_____ **1.** "I'll read it again to be sure there aren't any typos."

_____ **2.** "Do I have another memo that I can use as a model?"

_____ **3.** "I'll write down my thoughts and fix problems later."

_____ **4.** "I'll put the memo in my boss's Inbox so she sees it."

_____ **5.** "What's the goal of this memo?"

_____ **6.** "Does it make sense? Is everything organized well?"

_____ **7.** "Where can I find facts about the customer's order?"

MANUFACTURING: Rubin is a maintenance mechanic for Prime Processors, a company that makes and packages pastry fillings. When Rubin came on shift, his supervisor gave him a work order report that he had printed from a computer. The report tells Rubin what work to do on a machine.

Communication Strategies

Below is the report that Rubin gave to his supervisor after working on the machine. Read the form; then answer the questions that follow.

PRIME PROCESSORS
WORK ORDER PRINT REPORT

5/5/98

Work Order #: 0000704 (PM)   Task: *PREVENTIVE MAINT.*
INSPECT FOR WORN, LOOSE, OR DAMAGED PARTS. CHECK LUBRICATION. CLEAN.

Equipment #:   *108*   Warranty Expires: *2000*
EQ Description: *STEAM BOILER*
Location: *BOILER ROOM*
Department: *PLANT*   Current Meter: *None*
Cost Center: *73-13-0*

Originator: *Maintenance supervisor*   Request Date: *5-5-98*
Phone: *383-9900*   Extension: *54*

Start Date: Craft: *MECH*
Finish Date: Crew Size: *1*
Priority: *2.00*   Est. Labor Hours: *1.50*
Down Time: *1.50*

LABOR

Employee #: *38*   Craft: *MECH.*
Name: *RUBIN DIAZ*   Hrs: *1.50*

COMMENTS

Comments: *CHECKED FOR LEEKS. GREESED MOTOR PUMP.*
GREESED VALVES MECHANISMS. CHECKED WATER GUAGE.
Notes: *WORKING GREAT*

---

1. How does the work order report help Rubin do his job? Rubin uses it to

   a. _____

   b. _____

2. How does the work order report help the supervisor do his job? The supervisor uses it to

   a. _____

   b. _____

3. In what format is the work order report: memo, letter, or form? How does this format help ensure the report is accurate, well organized, and easy to read?

   _____

   _____

4. Did Rubin fill out the work order report accurately? Explain.

   _____

   _____

5. Which step in the writing process (see page 97) should Rubin follow to do a better job of filling out reports in the future? Explain why the step would be helpful.

   _____

   _____

COMMUNICATE

Imagine that you are Rubin's supervisor. On a separate sheet of paper, write a short conversation in which you explain to Rubin how to do a better job of filling out his work order reports. Be sure to follow the Problem-Solving Checklist presented at the top of Reference Handbook page 188. Use the format below:

Supervisor: Rubin, you did a good job on the boiler.
Rubin: Thanks, boss.
Supervisor: But,

Understanding Workplace Writing

The video program opened with a memo traveling from person to person in an ad agency office. You heard different people asking whom the memo was for, whom it was from, and what it was about. These questions point out three major characteristics of business writing. It has a purpose, contains facts, and often gives instructions to be followed.

A work team leader wrote the following statements for a memo to other team members. The purpose of the memo is to inform team members of her planned absence. Write _H_ next to each statement that <u>h</u>elps fulfill the purpose, gives a fact, or relates to an action. Write _DNB_ next to statements that <u>d</u>o <u>n</u>ot <u>b</u>elong in the memo.

_____ 1. Next Monday and Tuesday, January 9 and 10, I will attend a seminar in nearby Westmont.

_____ 2. I was hoping to be out of the building through Wednesday, but no such luck.

_____ 3. The seminar will present ideas on how to prepare our assembly line for the new equipment we are getting.

_____ 4. In my absence, José will serve as team leader.

_____ 5. If any problems arise, please bring them to José's attention.

_____ 6. I certainly hope this seminar is better than the last one.

Focusing on the Audience

The best business writing focuses on the needs of the audience—the person or persons who will receive the message. To persuade people to read your messages and take action, display a **"you" attitude.** Show the audience the benefits of taking the action you request.

"We/I" Attitude	**"You" Attitude**
We need your payment immediately.	Your prompt payment will protect your good credit rating.
I need your time card by 10 A.M. every Monday.	To ensure that your paycheck arrives on time, please turn in your time card by 10 A.M. every Monday.

On a separate sheet of paper, write at least three sentences to finish the following memo. Focus on what your co-workers need to know. Explain why they may need this workshop, how they will benefit from it, and what action they need to take to register for it.

To: All Employees   **Date:**
Subject: "Writing for the Audience" Workshop
From:

I am pleased to announce the next workshop of our "Business Writing in the 21st Century" series. The workshop will be held on Friday, November 14, from 3 to 5 in the boardroom.

Ensuring the Material Is Well Presented

After you have written a first draft, revise it. Check for the following as you reread your writing:

Revision Checklist

- ☐ Is the purpose of the message clear? Can the reader tell what to do?
- ☐ Does the message stick to the main point?
- ☐ Is the message well organized?
- ☐ Does it sound courteous and businesslike?
- ☐ Does it indicate whether a reply is needed?
- ☐ Does it have a "you" attitude?
- ☐ Is it neatly written or typed?

Use the checklist to revise the memo you completed above. Rewrite the memo on a separate sheet of paper so that you can answer "yes" to every question.

MANUFACTURING: Corliss is a shipping and receiving clerk for Topnotch Appliances. On November 23, she received returned merchandise from a customer. The following letter was enclosed with the merchandise.

Communication Strategies

Read the letter, and then follow the instructions on the next page.

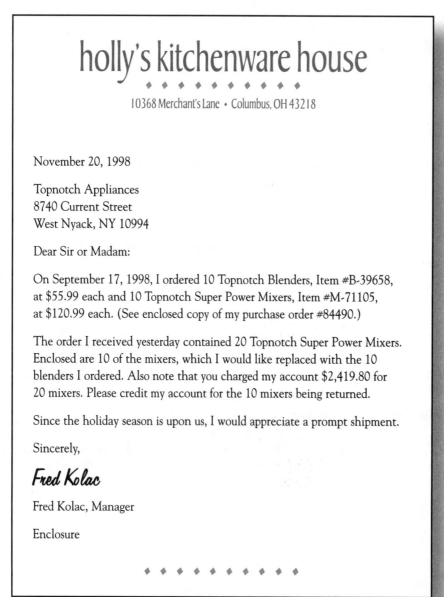

holly's kitchenware house
◆ ◆ ◆ ◆ ◆ ◆ ◆ ◆ ◆
10368 Merchant's Lane • Columbus, OH 43218

November 20, 1998

Topnotch Appliances
8740 Current Street
West Nyack, NY 10994

Dear Sir or Madam:

On September 17, 1998, I ordered 10 Topnotch Blenders, Item #B-39658, at $55.99 each and 10 Topnotch Super Power Mixers, Item #M-71105, at $120.99 each. (See enclosed copy of my purchase order #84490.)

The order I received yesterday contained 20 Topnotch Super Power Mixers. Enclosed are 10 of the mixers, which I would like replaced with the 10 blenders I ordered. Also note that you charged my account $2,419.80 for 20 mixers. Please credit my account for the 10 mixers being returned.

Since the holiday season is upon us, I would appreciate a prompt shipment.

Sincerely,

Fred Kolac

Fred Kolac, Manager

Enclosure

◆ ◆ ◆ ◆ ◆ ◆ ◆ ◆ ◆

Corliss has returned the 10 mixers to inventory and prepared 10 blenders for shipping. Now she has to fill out a Credit Request form for the accounting department so that the customer's account can be credited. Use the details in the customer's letter on page 102 to complete the form. Do whatever calculations are needed to ensure the customer is charged the right amount.

T O P N O T C H T A A P P L I A N C E S

Credit Request for Returned Merchandise

Date Received: _____ **Purchase Order #:** _____

Customer Name: _____

Address: _____

City: _____ **State:** _____ **ZIP:** _____

Item	Item #	Price	Quantity	Total Price

COMMENTS **Date:** _____

Reason for Return: _____

_____

Action Needed: _____

Shipping/Receiving Clerk: _____

COMMUNICATE

Imagine that you are the sales representative who handles the Holly's Kitchenware account. You have just received a copy of the letter on page 102. Holly's is a major account with billings in the thousands of dollars each year. Write three points you will make when you call the manager to ensure that he is satisfied after the shipping error is corrected. One point is listed for you.

1. Calling to apologize

Using Appropriate Language

When people are at home or outside the workplace, they are usually informal. They often dress casually, and they may relax their manners and language a bit. At work, however, clothing, manners, and language should be more formal. As the video program showed, the language used in written communication should be more formal, too.

To use formal language, avoid slang expressions that you might use with your friends. Also avoid business jargon, such as "please remit." Say "please send" instead. Simple, clear language is easier to understand. Finally, avoid technical **jargon** that is special to your industry. Jargon is expected when you're writing to someone in your specialty, but it is too technical and confusing to use when you're writing to customers and clients.

Classify each phrase and sentence. Write *Formal* for formal language, *Slang* for slang, and *Jargon* for jargon.

_____ 1. Everything's cool.

_____ 2. Everything is satisfactory.

_____ 3. I will endeavor to resolve...

_____ 4. Here's what went down...

_____ 5. Very truly yours,

_____ 6. Welcome to our...

_____ 7. I will be delighted to...

_____ 8. You are in arrears.

_____ 9. Enclosed please find...

_____ 10. I have enclosed...

Writing Clearly

What do people mean when they say, "Your writing isn't clear"? Generally, they are saying that they were confused by your writing and didn't understand your message. You can write more clearly by being straightforward, or direct, in your workplace communications. The chart on the next page offers some helpful tips.

> **How to Write Clearly**
>
> **State your purpose or position.** Describe the main point of your writing. Tell the reader what the communication is about or what your position is on a particular issue.
>
> **Use specific examples.** Give evidence to support your main point. Write down facts and examples to support it.
>
> **Make your case.** Explain *why* you made a certain decision or feel as you do.
>
> **State your desired response.** Clearly explain what it is that you want to happen. Tell how you want the reader to respond.
>
> **Reread what you've written.** Reread each sentence. Think about how the reader may interpret what you've written. Make changes to be sure your writing says what you want it to say.

Use the tips above to evaluate the letter on page 102. On a separate sheet of paper, explain whether the letter follows each tip. Give specific examples to support your evaluation. The first tip is done for you.

State your purpose: Mr. Kolac clearly states the purpose of the letter and explains what he wants to happen.

Checking Grammar and Usage

Once you've gotten your thoughts down on paper and revised them to make sure they are clear and appropriate, proofread to see if you made any of the following common errors. (For a brushup, see the checklists on pages 193–194.)

- Sentence fragments, or incomplete sentences
- Run-on sentences, or sentences not separated by a period
- Verbs and subjects that don't agree, such as "She *don't*"
- Pronouns and antecedents that don't agree, such as "Everyone has *their* faults."
- Lack of transitions, or connectors, such as *therefore* and *because*
- Misspelled words and problems with capitalization and punctuation

Proofread the memo you finished on page 101. Refer to the checklists on pages 193–194.

SERVICE: Mark Wilton is a sales representative for Grand Communications, Inc., a company that installs intercom and buzzer systems in apartment and office buildings. A new customer called Mark for a bid to see how much it would cost to install a new intercom entry system in an apartment building. As Mark walked through the building with the property manager, he wrote notes about materials that would be needed. When he got back to the office, he calculated the cost of parts and installation.

Communication Strategies

Read Mark's notes below. Then answer the questions on the next page.

From the desk of…
Mark Wilton

<u>Intercom Installation for</u>:

Owen Schwartz, Manager
Courtland Apartments
400-414 Maple Street
Elmhurst, IL 60126

<u>Special Details</u>:
- Wants a completely new intercom entry system.
- 45 apartments in building; 7 lobby entries; 1 front gate entry.
- Amplifiers will be installed in basement under each of the 7 lobby areas.
- Wiring will be done in a neat manner.
- Warranty on labor and material for two years.

<u>Materials and Labor</u>:		<u>Cost</u>:
(45)	2805 Intercom panels with surface back boxes	$1,000.00
(7)	3705 Dual lobby intercom control amplifiers	1,680.00
(7)	1088 16VAC transformers	2,100.00
(7)	4400 Lobby panels with frame and metal buttons	700.00
(1)	7743 Gate lobby equipment	2,100.00
	TOTAL	$7,580.00

<u>Payment Requirements</u>:
- 1/2 of total as a down payment.
- Balance due when system is operating correctly.

Help Mark to write a first draft of a letter from the notes he took.

Dear Mr. Schwartz:

[Purpose of letter] _____
_____
_____

[Special details] _____
_____
_____
_____

[Cost of materials and labor] _____
_____
_____
_____
_____
_____
_____

[Payment requirements] _____
_____
_____

[Your desired response] _____
_____

Very truly yours,

Mark Wilton

Mark Wilton
Sales Representative

READ IT

Mark knows that his customer won't be impressed if the letter has spelling mistakes in it. Proofread the draft you wrote above. Look at the spelling of each word. If you aren't positive that a word is spelled correctly, look it up in a dictionary. Read the definition of the word in the dictionary to be sure you are using the word correctly.

Review

Reading about how to write more effectively in the workplace is only a starting point for becoming a better communicator. To improve your skills, you must apply what you read. In this review, you will work on reviewing and proofreading a written business message.

Read the sample business writing below. Then answer the questions in the Review Checklist on the next page to evaluate this first draft.

Quality Home Contractors

2681 N. Long Avenue • Chicago, Illinois 60657
773-499-7997 • FAX 773-499-7998

FAX TRANSMITTAL

TO: _Kathie Zeco Sales Representative_

FROM: _Dittmar Schaefer Product Representative_

DATE: _October 23, 1998_

SUBJECT: _Defective Siding_

MESSAGE: _How you doing? How's things back at the office? Are our favrite customers, the Newmans, still upset about the defective siding? (Tell them to get a life!) Anyway, I got some answers. Attached is a copy of the letter we got today from Profit Products' quality control cordinator, Joe Mardean. It explains why the siding was defective and what the company has done to correct the problem. It should help you get out of hot water with the Newmans. Just tell them what Joe told us and explain that we'll replace the bad stuff with good stuff free of charge sometime next week._

NO. OF PAGES INCLUDING COVER PAGE: ___2___

Dittmar Schaefer

REVIEW CHECKLIST

1. Answer the questions below to review the first draft. (If possible, work with a co-worker, family member, or friend.) When you answer *NO* to a question, cross out and revise the problem on the first draft on page 108.

   Yes No
   ☐ ☐ **a.** Is the purpose of the message clear? Can the reader tell what action to take?
   ☐ ☐ **b.** Does the message stick to the main point?
   ☐ ☐ **c.** Does the message contain all necessary facts and details?
   ☐ ☐ **d.** Is the message well organized?
   ☐ ☐ **e.** Does the message sound courteous and businesslike?
   ☐ ☐ **f.** Does the message display a "you" attitude?

PROOFREADING CHECKLIST

2. Answer the questions below to proofread your revision. When you answer *NO* to a question, cross out and correct the error on the first draft on page 108.

   Yes No
   ☐ ☐ **a.** Are all sentences structured correctly? (See the Using Correct Sentence Structure checklist on page 192.)
   ☐ ☐ **b.** Is correct grammar used? (See the Grammar Checklist on page 193.)
   ☐ ☐ **c.** Is correct punctuation used? (See the Punctuation Checklist on page 194.)
   ☐ ☐ **d.** Is every word spelled correctly? (Refer to a dictionary for correct spellings.)
   ☐ ☐ **e.** Is the first word of every sentence capitalized? Are days of the week? Months?
   ☐ ☐ **f.** Is the message set up on the page correctly? (See pages 195–196.)
   ☐ ☐ **g.** Is the message neatly handwritten or typed?

3. Write the final draft on the form below. When you are done, proofread the message one more time to be sure that it is neatly written, clear, businesslike, and free of errors. If possible, ask someone to proofread the final draft with you.

Quality Home Contractors

2681 N. Long Avenue • Chicago, Illinois 60657
773-499-7997 • FAX 773-499-7998

FAX TRANSMITTAL

TO: _____

FROM: _____

DATE: _____

SUBJECT: _____

MESSAGE: _____

_____

_____

_____

_____

_____

_____

_____

_____

NO. OF PAGES INCLUDING COVER PAGE: _____

Supplying Information: Directions, Forms, and Charts

OBJECTIVES

In this lesson, you will work with the following concepts and skills:

1. Writing information clearly and accurately
2. Filling out forms accurately and completely
3. Using charts effectively

The video program you are about to watch shows different types of short writing tasks. The program will help you to do these tasks better and faster.

While you watch the video, think about how important short writing tasks are. Look for times when misunderstandings result from mistakes in writing down messages and other information.

Every day you probably write short items like grocery **lists,** telephone messages, calendar dates, time sheets, notes, **to-do lists,** and **order forms.** What happens if you don't write these items clearly, accurately, and completely? You won't have the right phone number. You won't get all of the items on your grocery list. You'll go to an appointment on the wrong day. Follow the guidelines in the video to prevent these kinds of mistakes.

Sneak Preview

This exercise previews some of the concepts from Program 14. After you answer the questions, use the Feedback on page 113 to help set your learning goals.

MANUFACTURING: As a warehouse assistant for Rain Miser lawn sprinkling systems, you read Customer Order Picking Tickets, pick the items from the warehouse, and fill in each ticket to show what you've done. Imagine that you filled in the following ticket. **Read the ticket; then answer the questions on the next page.**

Rain Miser, Inc.
1326 Norwood Road, Itasca, IL 60143

CUSTOMER ORDER PICKING TICKET

PRINT DATE: *May 10, 1999*

CO. NUMBER	CUSTOMER SERVICE REP.	CO. REV. DATE	CUSTOMER P.O. NUMBER
RM-098572-003	*SUE*	*05/14/99*	HSI 16832-1

ITEM	ORDER QUANTITY	ISSUED QUANTITY
RM-SSP-8		
RAIN MISER SSP SERIES CONTROLLER	1	*1*
RM-SSH-1206		
RAIN MISER SPRAY SPRINKLER 6" HEADS	9	*8*
RM-MVC-4200		
RAIN MISER MASTER VALVE CONTROL	8	*8*

CUSTOMER NAME	HALLORAN & SONS, INC., LAWN SPRINKLER SYSTEMS
ADDRESS	8342 S. 15TH AVE.
	MAYWOOD, IL 60153
TELEPHONE	708-344-0000

NEEDED BY: 05/20/99

SHIP DATE: *5/20/99*   SHIP VIA: *Co. truck*

SHIPPED/DELIVERED BY:

INSTRUCTIONS/COMMENTS:
LOCAL DELIVERY TO CUSTOMER. CALL CUSTOMER FOR DIRECTIONS.
Irving Park Rd. east to 294 south to 290 east to 25th Ave. south to Roosevelt Rd. east to 15th Ave. north to 8342. On east side.

1. Why did you write on the picking ticket? Check each reason.

    ☐ **a.** To change the customer's address
    ☐ **b.** To show the number of items picked
    ☐ **c.** To warn about a safety issue
    ☐ **d.** To indicate the shipping date
    ☐ **e.** To write directions for delivery

2. How many valve controls did the customer order?

    _____

3. By what date does the customer want the order?

    _____

4. Why did you need to call the customer?

    _____

5. Will the customer receive the correct number of items? Explain.

    _____

Feedback

- If you got all of the answers right . . .   you have a basic understanding of directions, forms, and charts. While watching the video, focus on problems that occur when these items are incorrect.

- If you missed question 1 or 4 . . .   you need a better understanding of why to write down information.

- If you missed question 3 . . .   you need to work with forms.

- If you missed question 2 or 5 . . .   you need to work with charts.

Vocabulary for *Supplying Information: Directions, Forms, and Charts*

charts	sheets of information arranged in columns and rows
checklists	series of tasks or steps that can be checked off as they are done
columns	information arranged in lines going down a chart
forms	typed or printed documents with blank lines and spaces for insertion of requested information
headings	labels written or printed at the top of columns or before rows to identify information
instructions	steps or orders to be completed
invoices	lists of goods sent to a buyer showing the terms of a purchase (items, prices, amounts, shipping charges, etc.)
labels	slips of paper written on and attached to anything for identification or description
lists	series of items, names, words, or phrases
order forms	written requests for goods that someone wants to buy or receive
rows	information arranged in lines going across a chart
signs	boards that have been written on for advertising or informative purposes
to-do lists	lists of a series of tasks that need to be done

PBS LiteracyLink®

Now watch Program 14.

After you watch, work on:
- pages 115–130 in this workbook
- Internet activities at www.pbs.org/literacy

Supplying Information: Directions, Forms, and Charts

On the following pages, you will learn more about the issues discussed in the video program and have an opportunity to develop your skills.

Think About the Key Points from the Video Program

When you are doing short writing tasks at work, an employer expects you to:

- Write **labels**, **signs**, lists, **instructions, forms,** and **charts** to communicate and track information.
- Organize the information and write clearly.

When working with forms, you should:

- Learn about types of forms and their purposes.
- Fill out forms completely and on time.
- Read the forms carefully, and correctly gather information you need from them.

When you work with charts, you should:

- Become familiar with the different types of charts and their purposes.
- Learn how the charts are organized.
- Complete charts neatly, accurately, and promptly.

Writing Down Information

In the video program, you saw workers making labels and signs, writing instructions, making lists, charting appointments and supplies, and filling out forms. Short writing tasks like these are essential in any business, because they help to organize work and keep co-workers informed. For example, labels help identify equipment, supplies, products, and files. Labels and signs remind workers where to look for specific items. Signs can also warn workers and visitors about problem areas or dangerous conditions. When you make labels and signs or fill out information, be accurate and precise. You'll save yourself and others time and trouble.

List three short writing tasks that you did today. Explain how each task helped you to be more organized or better informed.

Short writing task	How it helped me be organized or informed

Tracking Information Through Writing

By writing **checklists** or to-do lists, you help organize yourself and keep yourself informed. Lists can help you track information, such as what supplies to buy, what orders have been placed, or what needs to be done.

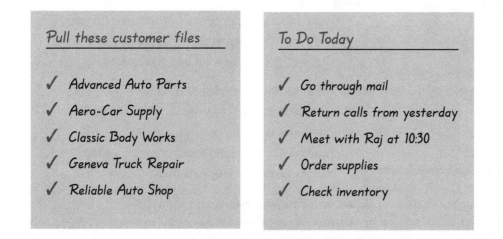

Pull these customer files

✓ Advanced Auto Parts
✓ Aero-Car Supply
✓ Classic Body Works
✓ Geneva Truck Repair
✓ Reliable Auto Shop

To Do Today

✓ Go through mail
✓ Return calls from yesterday
✓ Meet with Raj at 10:30
✓ Order supplies
✓ Check inventory

HOW TO REPLACE LEAKY SINK TRAP

1. Put pail under trap.
2. Unscrew locknuts holding trap to tailpiece and extension.
3. Remove old corroded pipe.
4. Stuff rag into drain pipe.
5. Install new trap.
6. Tighten locknuts.
7. Run water.
8. If leaky, remove trap. Put pipe joint compound on threads.

PLUMBING TOOLBOX CHECKLIST

✓ Propane torch
✓ Spud wrench
✓ Valve-seat wrench
✓ Standard pliers
✓ Basin wrench
✓ Hacksaw
✓ Pipe wrench
✓ Phillips screwdriver
✓ Standard screwdriver
✓ Tubing cutter

1. Describe two kinds of lists you have made at work or at home.

   _____

   _____

2. Explain how each list helped you be more organized.

   _____

   _____

Writing Clear Instructions

On the job, you may be asked to give instructions to a co-worker. Or you may need to give directions to a customer or client. When you do so, use exact and clear wording. Be specific. Use technical terminology when appropriate. When possible, write step-by-step directions, and put the steps in the order in which they should be done. Then check your instructions to make sure that they're clear, complete, and accurate.

On a separate piece of paper, write step-by-step instructions for an everyday task you do on the job or at home. Then have someone who needs to learn the job follow your instructions. Based on the person's feedback, make any necessary changes to the steps.

MANUFACTURING: Shanti works in a large home hardware store. Every six months she and her co-workers count every product in the warehouse to do inventory. Today, Shanti has to count all the kitchen sinks and faucets in the warehouse. She printed out a stock inventory report from the computer. The report lists every sink and faucet that has not been sold. Shanti knows that the numbers listed on the report may be different from the actual count because of mistakes in entering sales and returns into the computer.

Communication Strategies

Imagine that you are doing Shanti's inventory check. Use what you have learned about short writing tasks to help Shanti convey information.

Shanti checked all the aisles in the warehouse to find the boxes of kitchen sinks and faucets. She finally found them in Aisle 21.

1. In the box at the right, make a sign for Shanti to put at the front of the aisle so people know what they'll find on the shelves there.

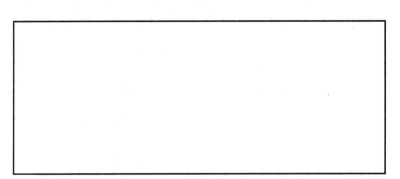

Shanti also needs to write labels to put on the boxes after she has counted them. Some boxes have labels from old inventory checks. Those labels say *Monday's Inventory Check* and *Checked Today*. Shanti thinks the labels should be more specific so when someone reads them later, the person will know exactly when the check was done and by whom.

2. In the box below, write a sample label that Shanti might use.

The following list is part of the stock inventory report that Shanti gave to her boss when she finished her check.

```
STOCK INVENTORY BY LOCATION                          09/06/1999
LOCATION DESCRIPTION: MAIN WAREHOUSE AREA 2

INVENTORY
ITEM              DESCRIPTION                        QUANTITY

✔ KSP-6050       SINGLE BOWL KIT SINK  8"  PORC      12
✔ KSP-6051       SINGLE BOWL KIT SINK 10"  PORC      07
  KSP-6052       SINGLE BOWL KIT SINK 12"  PORC      04   [5]
✔ KSS-6060       SINGLE BOWL KIT SINK  8"  ST STL    00
  KSS-6061       SINGLE BOWL KIT SINK 10"  ST STL    09   [7]
  KSS-6062       SINGLE BOWL KIT SINK 12"  ST STL    06   [4]
✔ KSP-6070       DOUBLE BOWL KIT SINK  8"  PORC      10
  KSP-6071       DOUBLE BOWL KIT SINK 10"  PORC      03   [5]
✔ KSP-6072       DOUBLE BOWL KIT SINK 12"  PORC      11
✔ KSS-6080       DOUBLE BOWL KIT SINK  8"  ST STL    14
✔ KSS-6081       DOUBLE BOWL KIT SINK 10"  ST STL    18
  KSS-6082       DOUBLE BOWL KIT SINK 12"  ST STL    07   [6]
✔ KFS-6070       1-HANDLE KIT FAUC ST STL            00
✔ KFS-6071       1-HANDLE KIT FAUC ST STL SPRAY      05
  KFS-6072       1-HANDLE KIT FAUC ST STL SOAP       00   [1]
```

3. How will Shanti's boss know that the quantity of an item listed on the report equaled the quantity of that item in the warehouse?

_____

4. What do the handwritten numbers in brackets stand for?

_____

5. When the quantity of an item is 5 or less, Shanti's boss will reorder that item. List the item numbers that will be reordered.

_____

MATH MATTERS ···

Figure out the difference between the total number of items on the printout and the actual total number of items. What problems might the difference in numbers cause? Write your answers on a separate sheet of paper.

Working with Forms

As the video program pointed out, you will fill out many different forms at work. Your first day at a new job, you might fill out tax withholding forms, medical history forms, and emergency information forms. Once you're on the job for a while, you'll fill out forms like vacation/time-off requests, medical forms, insurance forms, **invoices,** and overnight mail forms.

Make yourself a valuable employee. Become familiar with the different types of forms used at work and their purposes. Take the time to examine each form so that you can easily recognize common features, such as headings, directions, areas to be filled out, and places for signatures.

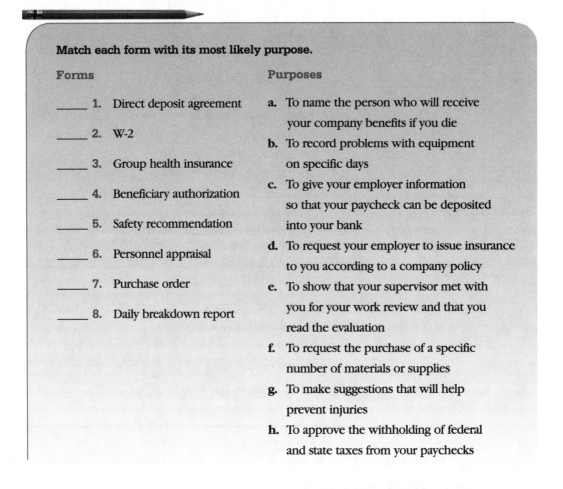

Match each form with its most likely purpose.

Forms	Purposes
_____ 1. Direct deposit agreement	**a.** To name the person who will receive your company benefits if you die
_____ 2. W-2	**b.** To record problems with equipment on specific days
_____ 3. Group health insurance	**c.** To give your employer information so that your paycheck can be deposited into your bank
_____ 4. Beneficiary authorization	**d.** To request your employer to issue insurance to you according to a company policy
_____ 5. Safety recommendation	**e.** To show that your supervisor met with you for your work review and that you read the evaluation
_____ 6. Personnel appraisal	**f.** To request the purchase of a specific number of materials or supplies
_____ 7. Purchase order	**g.** To make suggestions that will help prevent injuries
_____ 8. Daily breakdown report	**h.** To approve the withholding of federal and state taxes from your paychecks

Filling Out Forms

When you fill out forms at work, fill them out accurately and completely. Whoever reads the form later will not be able to read your mind to know what you meant. So be precise. Any mistakes you make will cost the company—and quite possibly you—money! The chart on the next page lists four strategies to help you fill out forms.

Strategies for Filling Out Forms

1. **Know your purpose.** Why are you filling out the form? If you don't know, ask someone who does.

2. **Know your deadline.** When does the form need to be handed in? A missed deadline may cost you some benefits or your company a sale.

3. **Make sure you have all the information you need.** Can you complete the form with the information you have? If not, get the information you need.

4. **Be careful, neat, and accurate.** Can someone else read what you've written? Did you write the information in the appropriate spaces? Did you proofread what you wrote?

On a separate sheet of paper, list the forms you need to fill out over the next month at work or at home. Next to each item on the list, write the purpose of the form, when it is due, and any items of information you will need to complete the form. An example has been started for you.

Example: Bank deposit form   **Purpose:** To add money to my account

Due: _____

Information: _____

Gathering Information from Completed Forms

Imagine that you're sending a package to a customer by overnight delivery. To completely fill out the mail form, you will need your company's overnight service account number; your company's name, address, and phone number; and the customer's name, address, and phone number. Where can you find this information quickly? Look at forms that have already been completed! You may find the information on an order form or service questionnaire the customer has completed, or on a recent mail form. The more familiar you are with different types of forms, the more time you'll be able to save.

Make a list of at least three forms you should save (originals or copies) for future reference. You may list forms you fill out at home, such as income tax forms, or forms you use at work.

_____

_____

_____

SERVICE: You are a billing clerk for Health•Rite, an exercise equipment manufacturer. After a customer's order has been picked, packed, and shipped, you receive a copy of the order form. You read it, enter items of information into a computer, and print out a detailed invoice of the items sold and total amount due.

Communication Strategies

Read the order form below; then fill out the invoice on the next page.

HEALTH•RITE
EXERCISE EQUIPMENT ORDER FORM

ORDERED BY:	SHIP TO:
Philip Friker	Philip Friker
CONTACT NAME	CONTACT NAME
Otus Office Center	Otus Office Center
COMPANY NAME	COMPANY NAME
3421 Market Street, Suite 2000	3421 Market Street, Suite 2000
ADDRESS, APT./SUITE #	ADDRESS, APT./SUITE #
San Francisco, CA 94114	San Francisco, CA 94114
CITY/STATE/ZIP	CITY/STATE/ZIP
415-325-0000	415-325-0000
PHONE	PHONE

ITEM #	DESCRIPTION	QUANTITY	UNIT PRICE
3057HPT	High Performance Treadmill	2	$649.99
27549ATS	Arctic Track Ski Machine	2	349.99
234HPS	High Performance Stepper	2	289.99

PACKED BY: *LM*

COMMENTS: *Entire order shipped. Sent by 3-day ground–Shipping & Handling charge $108.79*

Complete the form below. Fill in the billing and shipping information and the item number and description, quantity ordered, quantity shipped, and unit price information. (The information for the first item ordered has been entered for you.) Do not calculate the "Amount" or the information at the bottom of the form yet.

HEALTH•RITE
EXERCISE EQUIPMENT
2108 Wilshire Boulevard • Reno, NV 89557

DATE: 12/05/99

INVOICE NO. P47731

BILL TO:

SHIPPED TO:

ITEM # DESCRIPTION	QUANTITY ORDERED	QUANTITY SHIPPED	UNIT PRICE	AMOUNT
3057HPT High Perf. Treadmill	2	2	$649.99	$1,299.98

SUBTOTAL _____

SHIPPING & HANDLING _____

TOTAL _____

Use a calculator to compute the amount for each item ordered. Then add all of the amounts to get the subtotal. Find the shipping and handling charges listed on the order form. Enter it on the appropriate line on the invoice. Then compute the total amount due for this order by adding the subtotal and shipping and handling.

Using Charts Effectively

In the video program, you saw a number of charts—information arranged in **columns** and **rows.** For example, you saw calendars, schedules, price sheets, and time cards. At work, you may also use a variety of other types of charts. As with lists and forms, it is important to understand the purpose of any chart you use.

1. Name a chart you have used during the past week.

   _____

2. Describe the purpose of the chart.

   _____

3. What other charts might you use at home or at work?

   _____

Learning How Charts Are Organized

As mentioned before, the information in charts is arranged in rows and columns. Usually, **headings** describe the content of the columns and rows. To find the information you need or to fill in information, find the headings you want. Then move down and across to the box where the column and row meet.

Read the following employee schedule. Then answer the questions on the next page.

PART-TIME EMPLOYEE SCHEDULE FOR WEEK OF 12/8							
Name	Sun.	Mon.	Tues.	Wed.	Thurs.	Fri.	Sat.
Marta	X	9–4	10–5	3–7	X	9–1	9–12
Luke	10–3	X	9–4	10–3	11–5	11–3	9–12
Peter	X	11–4	9–4	X	12–4	9–2	11–4
Nadia	12–3	9–4	X	9–2	2–7	3–7	X
Emilie	10–3	3–7	3–7	X	9–4	X	12–5
Juan	X	3–7	X	11–4	2–7	9–4	12–5

1. On which day of the week are the fewest workers scheduled?

   (1) Sunday
   (2) Tuesday
   (3) Thursday
   (4) Saturday

2. Which employee works on Sunday, Monday, Tuesday, Thursday, and Saturday?

   (1) Luke
   (2) Peter
   (3) Nadia
   (4) Emilie

3. What time is Juan scheduled to work on Friday?

   (1) 10:00 A.M. to 3:00 P.M.
   (2) 9:00 A.M. to noon
   (3) 3:00 A.M. to 7:00 P.M.
   (4) 9:00 A.M. to 4:00 P.M.

Completing Charts

Follow these tips to fill out charts completely and accurately:
- Know the purpose of the chart; read the headings.
- Know when the chart is due; allow enough time to do an accurate job.
- Gather all the information you need before filling out a chart.
- Proofread the chart when you've completed it.

Use the schedule on page 124 to answer the following questions.

1. The purpose of the chart is to

   _____

2. List two pieces of information the person who filled out the chart needed to gather before completing it.

   _____

   _____

3. What is the last date by which the chart should have been completed and displayed?

   _____

WorkSkills

SERVICE: Miguel has worked for a Florida citrus grove for twenty years. Each growing season produces fruit for eight months of the year. Years ago, Miguel made the following list to help him remember which fruits would be ripe for picking each month.

Communication Strategies

When to pick fruit–

November: new tangelos, navel oranges, juice oranges, ruby red grapefruit, pink grapefruit, white grapefruit

December: new tangelos, navel oranges, juice oranges, ruby red grapefruit, pink grapefruit, white grapefruit

January: navel oranges, juice oranges, honeybell tangelos, ruby red grapefruit, pink grapefruit, white grapefruit

February: navel oranges, juice oranges, honeybell tangelos, temple oranges, ruby red grapefruit, pink grapefruit, white grapefruit

March: juice oranges, temple oranges, honey tangerines, ruby red grapefruit, pink grapefruit, white grapefruit

April: juice oranges, honey tangerines, valencia oranges, ruby red grapefruit, pink grapefruit, white grapefruit

May: juice oranges, valencia oranges, ruby red grapefruit, pink grapefruit, white grapefruit

June: juice oranges, valencia oranges, ruby red grapefruit

The grove's customer service manager has asked Miguel to make a chart that shows which months each fruit is available. **Use Miguel's list to fill in the chart on the next page.** The months in which new tangelos are available have been filled in for you.

FRUIT SEASONS	Nov.	Dec.	Jan.	Feb.	Mar.	Apr.	May	Jun.
New tangelos	✕	✕						
Navel oranges								
Juice oranges								
Honeybell tangelos								
Temple oranges								
Honey tangerines								
Valencia oranges								
Ruby red grapefruit								
Pink grapefruit								
White grapefruit								

Use the chart to answer the following questions.

1. Which fruits are available for all eight months?

    _____

2. Which fruits are available for two months each year?

    _____

3. In which month are the most fruits available?

    _____

4. In which month are the fewest fruits available?

    _____

5. Would you rather read information from Miguel's list or from the chart? Why?

    _____

TECH TIP •

Below is a database form. A database uses electronic forms to collect and organize information related to a common topic. **Place Xs in the boxes that correspond to the months that pink grapefruit are available.**

Fruit Availability

PRODUCT: | Pink Grapefruit |

Nov	Dec	Jan	Feb	Mar	Apr	May	Jun
☐	☐	☐	☐	☐	☐	☐	☐

Review

Reading about how to write more effectively in the workplace is only a starting point. To improve your skills, you must apply what you read. In this review, you will work on reviewing and proofreading a form.

SERVICE: Anna works in the admissions office of Pleasant Convalescent Center, a short-term care home for people recovering from illness or injury. New patients must list items they are bringing with them. Anna is preparing to admit a new resident, Mr. Jerzy Kowalski. His daughter, Katarzyna Kowalski, e-mailed the following list to the center. Anna printed out the message so she could use it to fill out a form.

Incoming Message   **Page 1 of 1**

SUBJECT:	Personal belongings of Jerzy Kowalski
SENT:	January 8, 1999 1:05:20 PM
RECEIVED:	January 8, 1999 1:53:36 PM
FROM:	KATKOW@XYZ.org
TO:	anna@PCC.com

As we discussed on the phone, my father will be admitted to the center on the morning of Jan. 10. His address is 817 Collman Avenue, Grass Valley, CA 95945; his phone number is 916-555-8118.

My father is bringing these things with him:

1. 1 gold wristwatch
2. 2 pairs shoes (1 gym; 1 leather slipper)
3. 5 pairs underwear
4. 2 warm-up suits
5. 1 deck playing cards
6. 4 hardcover books
7. 1 gold wedding band
8. 1 pair eyeglasses
9. hygiene: 1 upper denture, 1 cleaner, 1 deodorant, 1 electric razor
10. 1 wallet with ID; no money or credit cards

Please call (916-555-2222) or e-mail if you have questions.

Thank you, Katarzyna Kowalski

Compare the form below to the e-mailed list on page 128. Then answer the questions below. You will revise the form on the next page.

PLEASANT CONVALESCENT CENTER

PATIENT'S PROPERTY INVENTORY FORM. COMPLETE THIS FORM FOR EVERY PATIENT ADMITTED TO THE CENTER.

Patient's name: _Katerzyna Kowalski_

Address: _871 collman avenue, grass valley, CA. 95945_

City: _____ State: _____ Zip: _____

Telephone: _916-555-2222_

IN CASE OF AN EMERGENCY, CONTACT:

Name: _Jerzy Kowalski_

Telephone: _916-555-18118_

Relation to patient: _father_

THE PATIENT HAS BEEN ADMITTED WITH THE FOLLOWING PERSONAL PROPERTY:

Jewelry: _1 gold wristwatch_

Electronics: _none_

Clothing: _2 pairs gym shoes_ _2 warm suits_
5 pairs underware

Miscellaneous: _1 deck playing cards_ _1 upper dentue and cleaner_
4 hard books _1 deodorent_
1 wallet _1 pair eyeglasses_

Patient's signature: _____ Administrator's initials: _____

---

1. Did Anna complete the form? _____

2. Did Anna copy all the facts accurately? _____

3. Are all words spelled correctly? (Refer to a dictionary if you need to.) _____

4. Are all words capitalized correctly? _____

5. Revise and correct any items that contained errors in the information on page 129.

PLEASANT CONVALESCENT CENTER
PATIENT'S PROPERTY INVENTORY FORM. COMPLETE THIS FORM FOR EVERY PATIENT ADMITTED TO THE CENTER.

Patient's name: _____

Address: _____

City: _____ State: _____ Zip: _____

Telephone: _____

IN CASE OF AN EMERGENCY, CONTACT:

Name: _____

Telephone: _____

Relation to patient: _____

THE PATIENT HAS BEEN ADMITTED WITH THE FOLLOWING PERSONAL PROPERTY:

Jewelry: _____ _____

_____ _____

Electronics: _____ _____

_____

Clothing: _____ _____

_____ _____

Miscellaneous: _____ _____

_____ _____

_____ _____

_____ _____

Patient's signature: _____ Administrator's initials: _____

Writing Memos and Letters

OBJECTIVES

In this lesson, you will work with the following concepts and skills:

1. Planning written communications with a purpose and audience in mind
2. Organizing and writing first drafts
3. Writing, proofreading, and distributing final drafts

In this video program, you will review the seven steps in the writing process:

1. Identify your **purpose** and audience.
2. Gather facts and organize your thoughts.
3. Select a format.
4. Write a first **draft.**
5. Review and revise the draft.
6. Proofread the final draft.
7. **Distribute** your writing.

You will also see examples of different formats for written business communication, such as letters, memos, and reports, and learn how to apply them.

While you watch the video, notice what the employees in each situation want to communicate. Ask yourself why they chose to write and what format they used.

At home and at work, there will be times when you will need to write to someone. The guidelines you learn in this program will help you write effective messages.

Sneak Preview

This exercise previews some of the concepts from Program 15. After you answer the questions, use the Feedback on page 133 to help set your learning goals.

CONSTRUCTION: You are a plumber for Ho V. Nguyen Plumbing, Inc. The owner left the following note for you.

Ho V. Nguyen Plumbing, Inc.

Tuesday, 1/9

Mr. Owen Geyer asked me to bid on a horizontal water pipe replacement job in an apartment building he owns at 813-825 Green St., Louisville.

At 3:00 tomorrow, he's having a walk-through. Please accompany Owen, write a rough proposal for the job, and give it to me by the end of the week.

Thanks—   H.V.N.

After the walk-through, you draft the following proposal for Ho.

MEMO   **Ho V. Nguyen Plumbing, Inc.**

```
Date:  1/18/99
To:    Ho V. Nguyen
From:  kmc
Re:    Proposal for Horizontal Water Pipe Replacement
       Mr. Owen Geyer, 813-825 Green St., Louisville, KY

I met with Owen on Wed. Here's my proposal:

1. Remove all 2-inch galvanized cold water lines from 825 to 813.
2. Remove all 1- and 1 1/2-inch hot water galvanized piping from
   825 to 817 (by storage tank).
3. Install new piping with L-type copper.
4. Install new 3/4-inch ball valves at each tap section.
5. Install new 1-, 1 1/2-, and 2-inch ball valves at each section.

Cost:  $18,645.00
```

Answer these questions based on the situation.

1. Why were the note and proposal written? Mark each purpose that applies.

   (1) to inform   **(2)** to explain   **(3)** to persuade

2. What format did you put your draft of the proposal in?

   (1) note   **(3)** memo
   (2) business letter **(4)** report

3. How did you organize the communication to Ho?

   (1) outline   **(3)** list
   (2) most important ideas first   **(4)** bad news first

4. Ho called and asked you several questions about the proposal. He then chose a format for the proposal and wrote the first draft. Which format should Ho have used?

   (1) memo   **(2)** business letter   **(3)** handwritten note

5. What should Ho do after he writes the first draft of the proposal?

   (1) send it to Mr. Geyer by mail or fax   **(3)** gather facts and organize his thoughts
   (2) call Mr. Geyer and read it to him   **(4)** review and revise the draft

Feedback

- If you got all of the answers right . . .   you have a basic understanding of writing letters, memos, and reports. While watching the video, focus on why workers communicate in writing.

- If you missed question 1 . . .   you need a better understanding of purposes for writing.

- If you missed question 2 or 4 . . .   you need to learn more about different types of formats.

- If you missed question 3 . . .   you need to learn more about patterns of organization.

- If you missed question 5 . . .   you need to learn more about the steps in the writing process.

Vocabulary for *Writing Memos and Letters*

business letters	formal written messages sent to customers or business associates
complimentary closing	a formal ending to a business letter, such as *Yours truly*
distribute	to send or deliver a written message to intended receivers
draft	a version of a written message
"five *Ws* and an *H*"	fact-gathering questions (*Who? What? Where? When? Why? How?*)
graphics	graphs, charts, tables, and other visual representations of data
organizational patterns	standard ways to organize a business message
purpose	a reason for writing (to inform, to explain, to persuade)
routine reports	reports that are completed on a regular basis
special reports	nonroutine reports

PBS
LiteracyLink®

Now watch Program 15.

After you watch, work on:
• pages 135–150 in this workbook
• Internet activities at www.pbs.org/literacy

Writing Memos and Letters

On the following pages, you will learn more about the issues discussed in the video program and have an opportunity to develop your skills.

Think About the Key Points from the Video Program

Any time you write at work:

- Think about your purpose for writing.
- Consider who the reader is and what he or she needs to know.
- Select and use the best format for messages and notes.

To communicate effectively:

- Identify your purpose and audience.
- Select an appropriate format and write a first draft.
- Review and revise your first and second drafts.

To select the best format to meet your purposes:

- Learn about the formats in which memos are written.
- Read well-written **business letters** to see how they are organized.
- Recognize the formats that are commonly used to organize reports.

Planning Written Communication

What did the employees in the video have in common? They all planned their communication before they wrote. One of the things they thought about was their purpose for writing. Some workers wrote to inform someone of something. Some wrote to explain details about something. Others wrote to persuade someone to see things from their point of view. Still others wrote for all three reasons. When you write, follow the effective writing process. Begin with step 1: Identify your purpose and audience.

Think of four written items—letters, notes, memos, or reports—that you have recently written or received. List each item and its purpose. An example is listed for you.

ITEM	PURPOSE
report from bank	to inform me of account activity

STEP 1: Identifying Your Purpose and Audience

Once you've identified your purpose, follow through and think about your reader. Is the person a supervisor? A co-worker? A customer? Try to see your message from this person's point of view.

Think of a business message that you need to write. The message could be for work or for "personal business." Then answer the following questions.

1. Whom are you writing to? For what purpose?

   _____

2. What is your relationship with this person? How will that relationship affect what you say? How you say it?

   _____

STEP 2: Gathering Facts and Organizing Your Thoughts

The next step in the writing process is to gather the facts your audience needs to know and organize your thoughts. To do this step, put yourself in the place of your reader and think about what details he or she needs to know. To make sure you don't miss any important facts, answer the **"five *Ws* and an *H*": *Who? What? Where? When? Why? How?***

Businesses consider fact gathering so important that they often give employees printed forms to help them gather information. For example, many businesses pass out telephone message pads that remind employees what information to get when they take messages for others. Details on the forms may include whom the message is for and from, what the date and message are, when the call was made, and what the caller's number is.

Label each of the underlined facts in the note below with the question it answers: *Who? What? Where? When? Why? How?* **The first one has been done for you.**

1. When? ——————→ <u>Feb. 12</u>

2. _____

<u>Jan</u>

    Corrine Baber at Baber Design needs these kitchen <u>blueprints</u> tomorrow morning.

3. _____

4. _____

Please <u>ship them overnight</u> to her. Her address is <u>in my Rolodex</u>.

5. _____

Add a note asking her to call me <u>so we can go over them together</u>.

6. _____

Craig

RETAIL: Pete works in the men's coat department of a large retail store. He happens to be at the sales counter when the telephone rings.

Communication Strategies

As you read the dialogue below, imagine that you are Pete listening to the caller on the telephone. Then answer the questions on the next page.

Pete: Brother's Department Store. This is Pete in Men's Coats speaking. How may I help you?

Caller: Pete, my name is Lucita Grey. I was in your store two weeks ago and saw a leather jacket for my husband. Your store didn't have the size I needed. But the clerk checked with the Lakeside, Michigan, store and they had it. They were going to send it right away, but I haven't gotten it yet.

Pete: Let's see if we can track it down. Do you happen to know the merchandise and style numbers for the jacket?

Caller: Yes, the clerk wrote everything down for me. The merchandise number is 4591459, and the style number is 31751.

Pete: That was 4591459 and 31751, right?

Caller: Yes. The jacket is dark brown leather and zips up the front. It was on sale for $200.

Pete: How did you pay for the jacket?

Caller: I put it on my credit card.

Pete: And where was the jacket being shipped?

Caller: To my daughter's house. The jacket is a surprise for my husband's birthday. Let's see . . . Her address is 6333 Arnold, Westmont, IL 60126.

Pete: That's 6333 Arnold, Westmont, IL 60126. OK, Ms. Grey. I'll pass this information along to Ms. Jackson, the manager of the department, and have her call you back as soon as possible. Is there a phone number where we can reach you?

Caller: Sure, I'll give you my work number. It's 555-991-3377.

Pete: That's 555-991-3377. We'll get right on this, Ms. Grey.

Caller: Thanks a lot, Pete. I really want this jacket.

Pete: We'll see what we can do and call you later today. Good-bye.

1. On the form below, write down the facts Pete gathered during the telephone conversation. Use the current date and time to fill out the form.

IMPORTANT MESSAGE

FOR _____

DATE _____

M _____

OF _____

PHONE NUMBER _____

☐ Telephoned you   ☐ Please return call

☐ Visited you   ☐ Caller will call again

☐ Returned your call   ☐ URGENT

MESSAGE : _____

_____

_____

_____

_____

_____

SIGNED _____

2. Why did Pete repeat certain facts that Ms. Grey stated?

_____

MATH MATTERS ....

Use a calculator to figure the percent markdown on the jacket. The original price was $300, and the sale price was $200. First, find the difference between the original price and sale price. Then, calculate the percent markdown. To do this,

- enter the difference in the calculator
- press the division key [÷]
- enter the original price
- press the equals key [=]
- change the decimal to a percent

Organizing and Writing First Drafts

The writing process can help you organize and write business messages. Once you have identified your purpose and audience (step 1) and gathered and organized facts (step 2), you are ready to move to step 3 and select a format.

STEP 3: Selecting a Format

The three major formats in which business messages can be written are memos, letters, and reports. A memo is a brief message from one co-worker to another, often written on a special memo form. Business letters are usually used to communicate with people outside the workplace, such as customers and business associates. Reports are generally used to communicate technical data and findings to other employees or "outsiders."

> **Think of a business message you have recently written or received. On a separate sheet of paper, describe the purpose, the format used, and the reasons for using that format.**

Looking at Memos, Letters, and Reports

Memos begin with four headings (*To, From, Subject, Date*) and end with a brief message explaining the subject. (See the sample memo on page 195.) Because memos are a kind of form, they are a quick way for employees to **(1)** make requests of each other; **(2)** give instructions to each other; **(3)** make announcements; **(4)** notify each other of changes in policies. Memos can be written on paper or typed as e-mail.

Business letters are usually more formal in tone and appearance. They begin with a salutation, such as *Dear Sir*, and end with a **complimentary closing**, such as *Sincerely yours*. (See the sample letter on page 196.) Letters are a good way to: **(1)** make or answer a request or complaint; **(2)** confirm an agreement or a conversation; **(3)** thank someone.

Routine reports are usually written on forms. Short written work narratives (in which employees report work on a project) and accident or incident reports (in which employees explain the circumstances that led up to and followed an accident) are often completed this way. Although **special reports** are not written on forms, they do follow a pattern. They begin with a description of purpose, then present facts in writing and in **graphics**.

Which format would be best for each of the following messages?
Write *Memo* if a memo would be best; *Letter* if it should be a letter;
and *Report* if it should be a report.

_____ 1. A reminder to follow the company dress code

_____ 2. A record of how a customer was injured

_____ 3. A "thank you" to a client

STEP 4: Writing a First Draft

After selecting a format, you can begin step 4: write a first draft. During this step, you select a pattern of organization and then jot down your message. The chart below shows two major organizational patterns.

Good or Neutral News	Bad News
Uses: Presenting favorable news or news that is not likely to be upsetting, such as: • Announcements • Routine requests • Request for a job • Reminders • Thanks • Saying yes to requests	**Uses:** Presenting unfavorable news that is likely to be upsetting, such as: • Negative announcements • Complaints • Past-due notices • Saying "no" to requests
Pattern 1. State your purpose. 2. Present necessary facts and details. 3. Explain actions the reader should take and/or express thanks.	**Pattern** 1. State neutral news. 2. State the bad news, giving reasons for the negative situation. 3. State the action to be taken, if any, and end on a positive note.

Choose the best pattern of organization for each situation listed below. Write *G* for good or neutral news or *B* for bad news.

_____ 1. wedding announcement   _____ 3. refusal of scholarship

_____ 2. overdrawn bank account   _____ 4. mortgage approval

RETAIL: Tomas Barca is a stock clerk for A Piece of Europe gift shop, 1337 W. 55th Street, Stahlstown, PA 15687. He receives, unpacks, and checks all merchandise coming into the store. Six of the ten figurines he just unpacked are damaged. He reported the problem to his boss. Now he must write to the distributor, Imports Inc., 9645 S. Lincoln Avenue, Baltimore, MD 21218, and explain the problem. He will tell the distributor's customer service representative, Angela Wright, what action to take.

Communication Strategies

Help Tomas communicate the information above.

1. What is Tomas's purpose for writing?

    _____

2. What format should he use—memo, business letter, or report?

    _____

3. What organizational pattern should he follow—good news or bad?

    _____

4. Below is the first draft of the message Tomas wrote. Because the message is just a first draft, Tomas did not bother to write in paragraphs. On the next page, copy the message as it is onto the word processor screen but divide it into paragraphs to put it in the proper format.

    This morning, we recieved the ten porcelain figurines that we ordered on the first of the month (Catalog No. 91875). Thanks a bunch for the prompt shipment. Too bad that when I unpacked the figurines I discovered that six of them were damage. The figurines are popular with our customers, so we would like them replace. Please issue a return authorization number, arrange for pickup of the damaged goods, and send us six replacements as soon as possible. Because the holiday shopping season is almost here, we need the replacements by the end of the month. We appreciate your prompt attention to this matter.

```
 File   Edit   View   Insert   Format   Font   Tools   Window   Help
━━━━━━━━━━━━━━━━━━━━━━━━━ Untitled1 ━━━━━━━━━━━━━━━━━━━━━━━━━



















 Page 1                    Normal
```

COMMUNICATE

When Angela Wright receives Tomas's letter, she decides to call the owner of A Piece of Europe and apologize for the problem. On a separate sheet of paper, list the main points Angela should make.

Writing and Distributing Final Drafts

As you saw in the video, first drafts should not be sent as is. Instead, they should be reviewed, rewritten, and proofread.

Answer the question.

Why is it important to review and rewrite first drafts?

_____

_____

STEP 5: Reviewing and Revising First Drafts

When you review a first draft, ask yourself these questions:

- Did I use the right format?
- Is the message logically organized?
- Did I include all necessary facts, details, and instructions?
- Is the language clear and appropriate to the audience?
- Is the tone businesslike and polite?

When possible, have someone else, such as a co-worker or supervisor, also review your draft. Then revise it until you can answer "yes" to each question.

Answer the questions above to review the draft you copied on page 143. For which questions did you answer _NO_? Why?

_____

STEP 6: Proofreading the Final Draft

When you have reviewed and rewritten your message, you have created a final draft—the version of your message that you are preparing to distribute. Before you distribute the message, complete step 6: proofread the final draft. During this step, look for problems in grammar, mechanics, and spelling. If possible, work with a partner. If you need to make corrections, be sure to type, word process, or neatly write the message over again.

Cross out and correct the three grammar and spelling errors in the draft on page 143.

STEP 7: Distributing Your Writing

The last step in the writing process is to distribute your writing. If your message is formatted as a memo, you might:

- Make photocopies and put a copy in each receiver's Inbox.
- Send it electronically, via e-mail.
- Post it on a company bulletin board used for announcements.

Business letters are generally sent through the mail. However, if the letter needs to reach the receiver very quickly, you might:

- Fax the letter.
- Send it electronically, via e-mail.
- Call a messenger service and have it hand delivered.
- Send it via overnight mail services.

Because routine reports are usually distributed only to co-workers, employees usually use the same distribution methods that they use for memos. Special reports that are to be sent to outsiders—such as annual reports, in which a business presents its accomplishments and financial condition—are generally sent through the mail.

How would you distribute each of the written messages below? Explain your choices.

1. A business letter that has to reach the reader by day's end

   _____

2. A special report for outside investors in the business

   _____

3. A memo announcing that an employee has been promoted

   _____

4. A routine narrative work report to co-workers

   _____

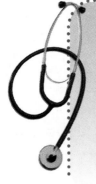

HEALTH CARE: Tanya Brobat is a school nurse. Lately, several children have come to her with injuries that they received on the school playground. On Monday, April 10, Bobby Feeny cut his knee so badly that he had to be sent to the emergency department of a nearby hospital. On Wednesday, April 12, Gilda Stein was sent to the hospital with a broken arm. Tanya completed accident reports on the children, but she wants to do more. She feels she can prevent further injuries by informing all the teachers of the accidents and reminding them to watch the children more carefully.

Communication Strategies

Follow the writing process to help Tanya write the message.

THE WRITING PROCESS

STEP 1. Identify purpose and audience.

1. What is Tanya's purpose for writing?

    _____

2. Who will receive the message?

    _____

STEP 2. Gather facts and organize thoughts (see page 137).

3. Use the "Five *W*s and an *H*" to list the facts that should be included in the message.

    _____

    _____

STEP 3. Select a format.

4. What format should Tanya use? Why?

    _____

STEP 4. Write a first draft.

STEP 5. Review and revise the draft (if possible, do this step with a partner, such as a co-worker, friend, or family member).

5. Here is Tanya's first draft. On the next page, revise the draft and put it in the right format.

    We seem to have a problem on our hands. Lately, more kids than usual have been getting hurt during recess. Some of the injurys were real bad. Bobby Feeny had to get stiches in his knee. Gilda Stein broke her arm. You need to watch your kids more carefully!

Write the revised message in the space below.

_____

_____

_____

_____

_____

_____

_____

_____

_____

_____

_____

_____

_____

_____

_____

_____

_____

_____

_____

STEP 6. Proofread the final draft.

6. Alone or with a partner, proofread the final draft above. Neatly correct any errors.

STEP 7. Distribute your writing.

7. Name two ways in which Tanya could distribute her message.

   a. _____

   b. _____

COMMUNICATE •

Suppose one of the teachers comes to Tanya complaining that he always watches the children carefully and "doesn't appreciate being accused of not doing his job." On a separate piece of paper, write what Tanya should say and how she should say it. (See the Problem-Solving Checklists on page 188-189.)

Review

Reading about how to write well in the workplace is only a starting point. To improve your skills, you must apply what you read. In this review, you will apply the effective writing process to write a job message.

SERVICE: You are looking for an entry-level office job. Today, you saw the following ad in the newspaper and decided to write a letter to apply for the job.

General Office Assistant
Busy law firm seeks full-time general office help. Answer phones, send and distribute faxes, make travel reservations, schedule meetings, photocopy. Willing to train. Good attitude and handwriting more important than experience. Send handwritten letter to: Ms. Fodor, Human Resources, TOWER & KING, c/o The Times. P.O. Box 620. Lexington, Kentucky 40502

Planning Written Communications (STEPS 1–2)

Answer these questions about the letter you will write.

1. Who is your audience?

   _____

2. What will your audience expect your letter to look like?

   _____

3. What is your purpose or purposes for writing?

   _____

4. Gather facts by answering the "Five *W*s and an *H*". (For questions that don't apply to you imagine that you are applying for this job.)

   a. **Who** are you? _____
   b. **What** job are you applying for? _____
   c. **What** are your qualifications? _____
   d. **Where** do you live? _____
   e. **When** can you be reached? _____
   f. **Why** does the job appeal to you? _____
   g. **How** can you be reached? _____

Organizing and Writing First Drafts (STEPS 3–4)

Answer these questions.

1. What format should you use?

   _____

2. Why should you use this format?

   _____

3. What pattern of organization should you use?

   _____

4. Why did you choose this pattern?

   _____

5. Use your answers to the questions above to write a first draft on a separate sheet of paper.

Writing and Distributing Final Drafts (STEPS 5–7)

1. Answer the questions below to review and revise the first draft. (If possible, work with another person.) When you answer *No* to a question, cross out and revise the problem on the first draft.

   Review Checklist

Yes	No	
☐	☐	Is the purpose of the message clear? Can the reader tell what action to take?
☐	☐	Does the message stick to the main point?
☐	☐	Does the message contain all necessary facts and details?
☐	☐	Are all facts and details accurate?
☐	☐	Is the message well organized?
☐	☐	Does the message sound courteous and businesslike?
☐	☐	Does the message display a "you" attitude?

2. Write your revised draft below.

_____
_____
_____
_____
_____
_____
_____
_____
_____
_____
_____
_____

3. Answer the questions to proofread your revision (if possible, work with another person). Make any corrections on the final draft.

Proofreading Checklist

Yes No

☐ ☐ Are all sentences structured correctly? (See the Correct Sentence Structure Checklist on page 192.)

☐ ☐ Is correct grammar used? (See the Grammar Checklist on page 193.)

☐ ☐ Is correct punctuation used? (See the Punctuation Checklist on page 194.)

☐ ☐ Is every word spelled correctly? (Refer to a dictionary for correct spellings.)

☐ ☐ Is the first word of every sentence capitalized? Are days of the week? Months?

☐ ☐ Is the message set up on the page correctly? (See pages 195–196.)

☐ ☐ Is the message neatly handwritten or typed?

4. How would you distribute your final draft? Explain your answer.

_____

Skills Review

Questions 1–8 are based on the following situation.

RETAIL: A customer who bought a stereo receiver from Yu has returned with the instruction booklet in hand.

Yu [*making eye contact*]: Good afternoon. Is something wrong?

Customer [*frowning*]: I bought a receiver here the other day, and I keep getting a buzzing sound whenever I listen to FM stations. I don't know what's wrong, and I can't seem to find an answer in the instruction booklet. Who writes these things?

Yu [*calmly*]: Do you hear the buzzing when you play CDs?

Customer: No. It's only with the FM radio.

Yu: It could be a problem with the FM antenna hookup. Let's look at the antenna on our showroom model. [*pointing to the FM antenna wires on the back of a receiver*] Is this how yours is hooked up?

Customer [*shaking head slowly*]: I don't remember anymore.

Yu [*smiling*]: That's OK. [*writing on a piece of paper*] I'll draw a diagram of how to hook it up. When you get home, compare the diagram to your FM wiring. If your wiring matches the diagram or if you switch the wiring but still hear the buzzing, call me at this number. We'll walk through some other possibilities over the phone. How does that sound?

Customer [*smiling*]: Great! Thanks a lot. I'll call if this doesn't work.

Write *True* if the statement is true; *False* if it is false.

_____ 1. Yu did not notice that the customer was upset.

_____ 2. Yu kept the discussion on track by ignoring the customer's comment about the writer of the instruction booklet.

_____ 3. Yu assumed he knew what was wrong and did not ask questions to find out if his hunch was correct.

_____ 4. The customer's shaking of his head was a nonverbal message that he was confused and frustrated.

_____ 5. When Yu asked, "How does that sound?" he was checking to see if the solution was satisfactory.

_____ 6. The customer showed he was listening when he said, "I'll call if this doesn't work."

_____ 7. Yu spoke in a negative tone of voice.

_____ 8. Yu communicated well with the customer.

Questions 9–11 are based on the following situation.

SERVICE: Sasha, a customer service representative, has received a call from a customer who bought a video game station. The customer didn't realize that the joystick was not included and wants Sasha to set one aside.

Sasha: We don't usually put items on hold, but since you've already bought the game station, I'll make an exception. What is your name?

Customer: I'm Rita Fuentes.

Sasha: I'm not working tomorrow, Ms. Fuentes, so I'll leave the joystick in the store manager's office. Her name is Nancy Lubner.

Sasha [*knocking on Nancy's door*]: Nancy, Ms. Fuentes, a customer, is coming in tomorrow to pick up this joystick. I put it on hold for her.

Nancy: Sasha, I've asked you before not to put things on hold.

Sasha: I know, but I didn't want to argue with a customer.

Nancy: I can understand that, but the policy is important. We're able to sell at a discount because we sell in volume. Often, customers don't pick up items on hold, and then we lose sales. Do you understand?

Sasha: Yes. I'm sorry, Nancy.

Choose the best answer to each question.

9.   Nancy gave feedback to Sasha to

    (1) remind her that store policy must be followed

    (2) assert her authority over Sasha

    (3) solve a customer problem

    (4) make Sasha sorry for doing the wrong thing

10. Nancy kept the communication on task by

    (1) sympathizing with Sasha

    (2) refusing to put the item on hold

    (3) explaining the reason behind store policy

    (4) ignoring Sasha's explanation

11. What cause for Sasha's actions did Nancy uncover?

    (1) Sasha is stubborn and refuses to follow orders.

    (2) Sasha thinks the policy is foolish.

    (3) Sasha is careless and forgetful.

    (4) Sasha is uncomfortable saying no to customers.

Questions 12–18 are based on the following situation.

MANUFACTURING: Matshi-Piker, a manufacturer of passenger jets, is behind schedule. Delivery of eight jets was promised by the end of the year, but with the holidays coming, production will be halted. The production manager has formed a team to work on a solution.

Manager: We'll lose millions if we don't meet this deadline. You're on the front line, so you know best the problems we face. Work together and find a solution that's satisfactory to everyone. [*Leaves.*]

Welder: Does he actually think we can meet this deadline?

Mechanic: I guess so. This is the biggest job our company has had in five years. Who knows what will happen if we don't finish the jets on time?

Sheet metal worker: That's true. It's in our best interest to come up with a good plan.

Mechanic: No one's going to be happy about it, but the only thing I can think of is to keep the plant open during the holidays.

Welder: What? Are you crazy? Our co-workers will never go for it!

Sheet metal worker: They will if we give them a good reason to.

Welder: Like what?

Sheet metal worker: For one, their jobs may depend on it. But maybe the company would offer an incentive—like double time.

Mechanic: Yeah! I know a few people who would go for it then.

Welder: Come to think of it, I might work through the holidays, too!

Write *True* if the statement is true; *False* if it is false.

_____ 12. The team goal is to develop a plan that will benefit the company, the customers, and the workers.

_____ 13. The welder refused to work with the team.

_____ 14. The mechanic took the initiative in problem solving.

_____ 15. The team appears to need a manager to lead it.

_____ 16. The workers are functioning as individuals rather than as a team.

_____ 17. The team should develop an alternative plan.

_____ 18. The team members kept their opinions to themselves.

Questions 19–21 are based on the following situation.

SERVICE: Felicia is a customer service representative for Harvest Festival, a mail order shipper of fruits. She is on the phone with a customer.

Customer: I just found out that one of my clients—probably all of them—received a fruit basket without my name listed as the sender. What good is it to send gifts if my clients don't know who sent them?

Felicia: Did you include your name in the message section of the form?

Customer: No. My name was preprinted on the order form, so I assumed you would automatically print my name on the order.

Felicia: I see your point, but you need to write your name in our message section if you want it to appear on the shipping form.

Customer: Well, why don't you point that out on your order form?

Felicia: That's a good suggestion, and I'll pass it on to my supervisor. As for your gift baskets, will it be sufficient if I send a letter to each recipient explaining that you are the sender?

Customer: Yes, that's fine. And please be sure to change your order form so people know to include their names in the messages!

Felicia: I'll see what I can do. Thanks for bringing this problem up.

Choose the best answer to each question.

19. The way Felicia handled the problem shows that she

    (1) understands the importance of customer satisfaction
    (2) feels the customer is at fault so she needn't do anything
    (3) wants to complete the call as soon as possible
    (4) is angry about the customer's suggestion

20. To provide for the customer's needs, Felicia

    (1) pointed out that no one else ever complained about the form
    (2) offered a solution and asked the customer if it was OK
    (3) explained why the customer was wrong
    (4) apologized but pointed out she could do nothing

21. Which of the following best describes Felicia's approach?

    (1) Find out who is to blame and tell the supervisor.
    (2) Tell customers whatever you think will make them happy.
    (3) Don't take responsibility for other people's mistakes.
    (4) Focus on solutions, and don't take criticism personally.

Questions 22–28 are based on the following message.

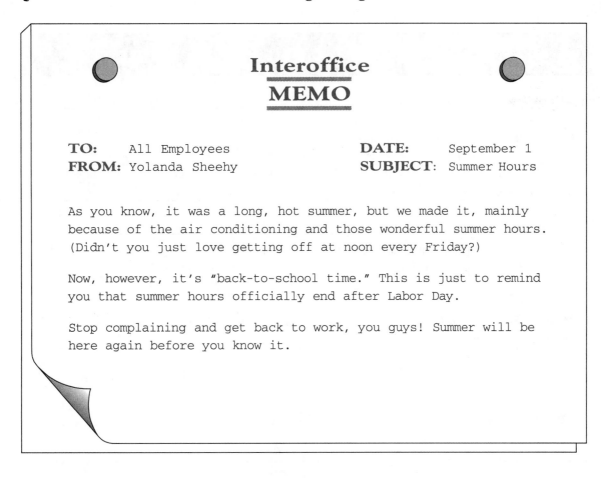

Interoffice MEMO

TO: All Employees

FROM: Yolanda Sheehy

DATE: September 1

SUBJECT: Summer Hours

As you know, it was a long, hot summer, but we made it, mainly because of the air conditioning and those wonderful summer hours. (Didn't you just love getting off at noon every Friday?)

Now, however, it's "back-to-school time." This is just to remind you that summer hours officially end after Labor Day.

Stop complaining and get back to work, you guys! Summer will be here again before you know it.

Write *True* if the statement is true; *False* if it is false.

_____ 22. The message is a type of business writing.

_____ 23. The message is formatted as a letter.

_____ 24. The message is written in formal language.

_____ 25. The purpose of the message is to inform employees of a change in work hours.

_____ 26. The message is organized according to the "bad news" pattern.

_____ 27. The writing is straightforward and businesslike.

_____ 28. The message focuses on the needs of the reader.

Questions 29–33 are based on the following written communication.

E M P L O Y E E   A C C I D E N T   I N Q U I R Y

Employee Name: *Elena Zeladon*   Date injury occurred: *1/4/99*

Describe the accident in detail (what, where, how it happened):
I cut the back of my left leg and needed 28 stitches. It happened at work as I was walking down the metal stairs
from the lunchroom. I slipped on a piece of paper and fell down 4 or 5 stairs. My leg got caught on a jagged edge of
one of the stairs.

Did you experience pain at the time of the injury? *Yes.*

If so, describe the pain and part(s) of the body injured at the time of the accident.
At first I felt a sharp shooting pain in my left leg. Then I felt a burning sensation. It hurt so much
that I cried.

COMMENTS: *The stairs should be cleaned so people don't get hurt. The rough edges of the stairs*
should be sanded down.

Elena Zeladon 2-5-99
EMPLOYEE SIGNATURE AND DATE

WERE THERE ANY WITNESSES? Yes ☒   No ☐

_____
WITNESS SIGNATURE AND DATE

Fill in each blank with the correct answer.

29. What is the purpose of the message?

_____

30. What format is the message in: form, letter, or memo?

_____

31. How does this format help the writer organize information?

_____

32. How does this format help the reader find information?

_____

33. What information is missing from the message?

_____

Questions 34–39 are based on the following letter.

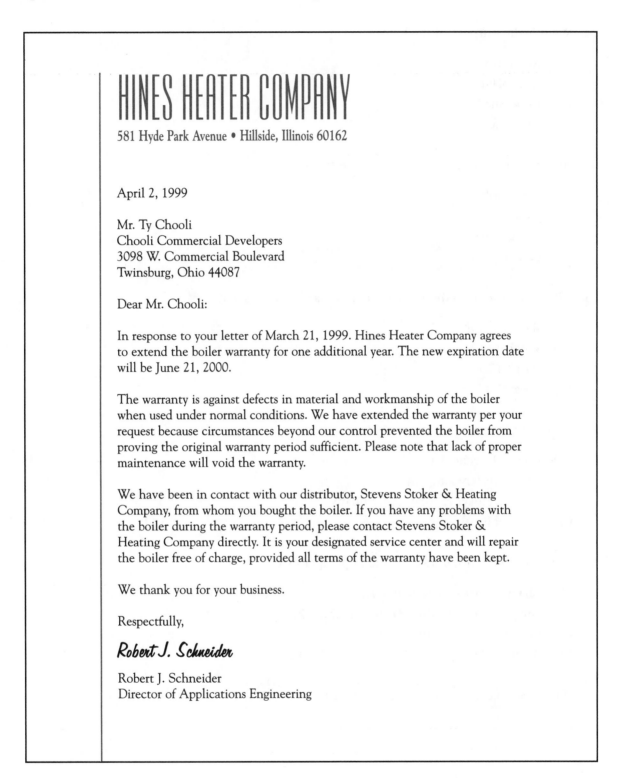

HINES HEATER COMPANY

581 Hyde Park Avenue • Hillside, Illinois 60162

April 2, 1999

Mr. Ty Chooli
Chooli Commercial Developers
3098 W. Commercial Boulevard
Twinsburg, Ohio 44087

Dear Mr. Chooli:

In response to your letter of March 21, 1999. Hines Heater Company agrees
to extend the boiler warranty for one additional year. The new expiration date
will be June 21, 2000.

The warranty is against defects in material and workmanship of the boiler
when used under normal conditions. We have extended the warranty per your
request because circumstances beyond our control prevented the boiler from
proving the original warranty period sufficient. Please note that lack of proper
maintenance will void the warranty.

We have been in contact with our distributor, Stevens Stoker & Heating
Company, from whom you bought the boiler. If you have any problems with
the boiler during the warranty period, please contact Stevens Stoker &
Heating Company directly. It is your designated service center and will repair
the boiler free of charge, provided all terms of the warranty have been kept.

We thank you for your business.

Respectfully,

Robert J. Schneider

Robert J. Schneider
Director of Applications Engineering

Choose the best answer to each question.

34. What is the purpose of the letter?

    (1) to inform
    (2) to explain
    (3) to persuade
    (4) all of the above

35. Where is the specific purpose of the letter stated?

    (1) paragraph 1
    (2) paragraph 2
    (3) paragraph 3
    (4) paragraph 4

36. Which questions do the facts in the first paragraph answer?

    (1) *When? Who?*
    (2) *Why? How?*
    (3) *Why? What?*
    (4) *Where? Why?*

37. Who is the recipient of this letter?

    (1) Robert J. Schneider
    (2) Hines Heater Company
    (3) Stevens Stoker & Heating Company
    (4) Ty Chooli

38. Which correction should be made in paragraph 1?

    (1) Change *warranty* to *warrenty.*
    (2) Omit the comma after *21* in *June 21, 2000.*
    (3) Correct the first sentence so it's not a fragment.
    (4) Remove the capital letters from *Heater* and *Company.*

39. What should the writer do after revising the letter? Why?

    _____

    _____

Skills Review Answer Key

1. False
2. True
3. False
4. True
5. True
6. True
7. False
8. True
9. (1) remind her that store policy must be followed
10. (3) explaining the reason behind store policy
11. (4) Sasha is uncomfortable saying no to customers.
12. True
13. False
14. True
15. False
16. True
17. True
18. False
19. (1) understands the importance of customer satisfaction
20. (2) offered a solution and asked the customer if it was OK
21. (4) Focus on solutions, and don't take criticism personally.
22. True
23. False
24. False
25. True
26. True
27. False
28. False
29. to record the circumstances surrounding an accident
30. form
31. It tells what facts to include and where to write them.
32. All information is clearly labeled.
33. the signature of the witness
34. (4) all of the above
35. (1) paragraph 1
36. (1) *When? Who?*
37. (4) Ty Chooli
38. (3) Correct the first sentence so it's not a fragment.
39. proofread to make sure the letter is error-free

Skills Review Evaluation Chart

Circle the question numbers that you answered correctly. Then fill in the number of questions you got correct for each program lesson. Find the total number correct, and review the lessons you had trouble with.

Program Lesson	Question Number	Number Correct/Total
9: *The Language of Work* Speaking and Listening, Identifying Nonverbal Communication, Developing Effective Communication Skills	1, 2, 3, 4, 5, 6, 7, 8	____/8
10: *Communicating with Co-Workers and Supervisors* Communicating Successfully with Co-Workers, Communicating with Supervisors, Resolving Conflicts with Co-Workers and Supervisors	9, 10, 11	____/3
11: *Working Together* Developing Teamwork Skills, Participating on a Work Team, Being Part of an Effective Team	12, 13, 14, 15, 16, 17, 18	____/7
12: *Communicating with Customers* Understanding the Importance of Customer Satisfaction, Providing for Customers' Needs, Working with Difficult Customers	19, 20, 21	____/3
13: *A Process for Writing* Becoming an Effective Writer, Understanding Workplace Writing, Using Appropriate Language	22, 23, 24, 25, 26, 27, 28	____/7
14: *Supplying Information: Directions, Forms, and Charts* Writing Down Information, Working with Forms, Using Charts Effectively	29, 30, 31, 32, 33	____/5
15: *Writing Memos and Letters* Planning Written Communication, Organizing and Writing First Drafts, Writing and Distributing Final Drafts	34, 35, 36, 37, 38, 39	____/6
	Total	____/39

WHAT YOUR SCORE MEANS

If you got 36–39 correct: You have an excellent understanding of workplace communication. Your workplace communication skills will serve you well both in the workplace and in everyday life.

If you got 32–35 correct: You have a good understanding of workplace communication. See which topic areas the questions you missed belong to, and review these topics.

If you got 28–31 correct: You need to develop your communication skills in the workplace. See which topic areas the questions you missed belong to, and review these topics.

If you got fewer than 28 correct: You need to review the basic principles in each program. By reviewing the programs and doing the exercises in this book, you can gain the knowledge and skills you need.

Answer Key

PROGRAM 9: THE LANGUAGE OF WORK

Speaking and Listening, page 16

Answers will vary. Sample answers are as follows: Person: Jennifer; Subject: Scheduling problems; Effectiveness: Communication was effective. The schedule was revised to everyone's satisfaction.

Using Active Listening Strategies, pages 16–17

If you wrote *True* for any of the statements, you need to work on your active listening skills. Review the active listening tips in the chart, and apply them whenever you are in a listening situation.

Speaking Effectively, page 17

Answers will vary. Compare your answer to these sample reasons: Mr. Hernandez is an effective speaker because (1) he knows what he's talking about, (2) he always sounds enthusiastic, (3) he keeps the conversation on the subject, (4) he explains technical terms that I need to learn, and (5) he's always willing to answer my questions.

WorkSkills, pages 18–19

Answers will vary. Sample answers:

1. How will I know if the computer read my swipe card?
2. Should I count babies as guests, even though they won't be ordering?
3. If they don't want appetizers, I'd just touch "Dinners" or "Desserts," right?
4. If I press a wrong number, how do I correct it?
5. If I mistakenly send an incorrect order, should I tell the cook about it in person, or should I correct it in the computer and send the order again?

Write It, page 19

Answers will vary. Sample notes:

- Write order on ticket.
- Swipe my card at top of computer.
- Touch table number.
- Touch number of guests.
- Touch type of food ordered.
- Touch 1 for first guest.
- Touch button for specific food ordered.
- Repeat for each guest.
- Touch "Send."

Identifying Nonverbal Communication, page 20

1. confused
2. confident
3. impatient

Communicating through Gestures, page 21

2, 4, 5, 6, and 8 should be checked.

Using a Positive Tone of Voice, page 21

1–2. Answers will vary. If you listed qualities other than "calm and smooth" and "expressive," you need to work on developing a more positive tone of voice.

WorkSkills, pages 22–23

1. (4)
2. (2)
3. Answers will vary. Sample answer: Mai should smile and make eye contact with the guests as she greets them with a warm and friendly tone of voice. She should show an interest in their comments and questions.

Tech Tip, page 23

Answers will vary. Sample answers:

1. Good morning!
2. Thank you for calling the Majestic Hotel gift shop. This is Mai speaking.
3. How may I help you this morning?
4. Mai should answer the phone by the third ring. She should speak in a calm, smooth, and expressive tone of voice.

Developing Effective Communication Skills, page 24

Any behavior you checked can lead to a miscommunication. Work on correcting that behavior so you can communicate effectively.

Finding Common Ground, page 24

(2)

Using Problem Solving, page 25

Answers will vary. Compare your answers to these sample answers:

1. I got mad at a customer because she started yelling at me even though I wasn't the clerk who caused her problem.

2. I should have stayed positive and not made the negative comments that I made. I should have apologized for the problem even though it was not my fault, because I am a representative of the business when I am at work. I also should have showed the customer that I cared about her problem by asking questions to be sure I understood it. Finally, I should have asked the customer how she wanted the problem to be corrected. I should have asked my supervisor if I could do what the customer wanted.

WorkSkills, pages 26–27

Answers will vary. Sample answers:

1. a. She discussed the problem in private.

    b. She was honest that there was a problem.

    c. She asked questions to be sure Gladys understood what the problem was.

    d. She worked with Gladys to find a solution that was agreeable to both of them.

2. a. She might have rephrased her questions so that she didn't sound as if she were attacking Gladys.

    b. She might have spoken in a calmer tone of voice.

3. If Gladys told jokes about some other group, somebody else at work might be offended.

4. It was extreme. Gladys doesn't need to completely stop telling jokes.

5. for Gladys to stop telling ethnic jokes but to continue telling other jokes

6. Sample answer: You can miscommunicate even when you're trying to solve a problem. The key is to remain calm, be sure both parties know what the problem is, and work together to find a reasonable solution.

Write It, page 27

Answers will vary. Sample answer:

Carla: Rick, sometimes I feel as if you think I can't handle the responsibilities of my job.

Rick: Well, you are a little young to be a supervisor, aren't you?

Carla: I'm not that young, Rick. The important thing is, I have ten years' experience.

Rick: I'm sorry, Carla. I didn't realize that. The truth is, you look about the same age as my daughter, so I guess I see you as just a kid. Look, from now on, I'll just stay out of your way.

Carla: Could you maybe try to see me as I see myself instead? As someone who's proud of working her way up and eager to learn from more experienced co-workers?

Rick: I'll try, but it's hard. Sometimes you come off as kind of demanding. It's hard to take that from someone younger than myself. By the way, when you said "more experienced," was that a nice way of saying I'm old?

Carla: Not at all. I really meant what I said.

Rick: Would you like me to show you the ropes?

Carla: I'd really appreciate that. But you know, I always try to talk things over with you when I'm not sure what to do. Maybe the real solution is for you to let me know when you think I'm being too demanding, and for me to let you know when I feel you're looking down on me.

Rick: Fair enough.

The third solution—to be more honest and direct with each other—met both people's needs. The first solution was unacceptable because it didn't address part of the real problem: Rick's feeling that Carla was too aggressive. The second solution didn't address the entire problem either.

Review, pages 28–30

STEP 1: Apply Your Skills

Answers will vary. Sample answers:

1. I plan to talk to James.

2. I will talk to him tomorrow.

3. The purpose of the conversation is to set up procedures for mailing packages properly.

4. I would like for us to come up with a short, clear list of do's and don'ts for the department to follow.

STEP 2: Self-Evaluation

1. You should have answered *Yes* to items a–1. Make note of any statements you answered *No* to. These indicate the skills you need to improve.

Answers to questions 2–4 will vary. Sample answers:

2. The conversation was successful, because James and I created the list and the rest of the department made positive comments about it.

3. I think I listened especially well to James's point of view; his was different from mine because he's a mailroom clerk and I'm not.

4. I need to work on being aware of my nonverbal communication. I don't pay much attention to my facial expressions or gestures, but I should. I also need to remember to stick to the point of business conversations. I tend to start joking around and socializing.

STEP 3: Personal Action Plan

Answers will vary. Sample answers:

1. I will work on sticking to the purpose of conversations and sending positive nonverbal messages.

2. I will work to improve these skills from January 2 to January 12.

3. In my conversations, I will smile, make steady eye contact, stand up or sit up straight, and look interested in what the other person has to say. I will try to understand the other person's point of view.

4. I will keep track of my progress by keeping a communication journal.

5. By following the action plan, I learned to keep my conversations on target. I think people are listening to me more carefully now because of the way I'm listening to them. I also think people are taking me more seriously.

PROGRAM 10: COMMUNICATING WITH CO-WORKERS AND SUPERVISORS

Communicating Successfully with Co-Workers, page 36

Answers will vary. Any of the reasons may be checked. You may want to jot down other reasons that aren't listed.

Using Good Judgment, pages 36–37

Answers will vary. Sample answers:

1. Our boss forced the solution on us, so I was unhappy.

2. Asking the boss to step in was not the best approach. I should have tried solving the problem together with my co-worker. I also should have tried to see things from his point of view while working on the solution.

Keeping Workplace Communication on Task, page 37

1. 1 and 2
2. 2 and 3
3. 1 and 4
4. 2
5. 1 and 4

WorkSkills, pages 38–39

1. Zoya, would you be able to switch shifts with me next Thursday so I can go with my son on a field trip?

2. Gee, that's the day Jim and I are going to the Cubs game.

3. Could you go to a game on Wednesday or Friday instead?

4. I doubt it. Jim's already asked for the day off.

5. Please, Zoya. How many times have I switched shifts for you?

6. You're right. You've always been there when I needed to switch.

7. Thanks, Zoya! I really appreciate it!

Write It, page 39

Answers will vary. Sample answers:

(1) Juanita could ask her supervisor to intervene. **Cons:** Zoya will resent being told what to do, and she also might make things very difficult for Juanita in the future. **Pro:** Juanita will be able to go with her son.

(2) Juanita might ask someone else to switch shifts with her. **Con:** Everyone will say no. **Pro:** She gets what she wants.

(3) Juanita might take a personal day so she can go with her son. **Cons:** She will have one less personal day to use for other, perhaps more pressing, reasons. She's docked for the shift. **Pros:** She gets the day off. It might be best to ask someone else to switch shifts. If that fails, Juanita might ask for a personal day. Supervisors don't usually like getting involved in employee disputes. In any event, Juanita can let Zoya live with the consequences of refusing to switch shifts. The next time Zoya wants anything from Juanita, Juanita will be in control of the situation.

Communicating with Supervisors, page 40

Answers will vary. Sample answers:

1. a. to be social and ask how his weekend was

    b. to give him a status report on getting the customers' orders out

    c. to ask for help on a customer's request

    d. to ask him to prioritize the work

    e. to suggest a change in the procedures to follow in processing customers' orders

2. I could keep my supervisor better informed about our work progress. I could listen more carefully when my supervisor explains why we have to do things a certain way. I could ask more questions when I'm not sure about something. When I see a problem, I could suggest ways to correct it.

Taking Direction, pages 40–41

Answers will vary.

1. If you did not check off all five strategies, you need to develop those skills.

2. You should use any strategy that you did not check off in question 1. A good listener uses all five active listening strategies.

Responding to Feedback, page 41

1. False

2. True

3. True

4. True

WorkSkills, pages 42–43

1. (3)

2. (4)

3. (4)

4. (2)

5. (1)

6. (3)

Math Matters, page 43

$17,000 – $10,000 = $7,000 remaining on old order
$7,000 + $32,000 = $39,000 due on both orders
Trucko Brothers will owe $39,000.

Resolving Conflicts with Co-Workers and Supervisors, page 44

Answers will vary. Sample answers:

1. a. My supervisor yelled at me for being late.

    b. I was upset with a co-worker because she was distracting me from my work.

2. a. I had a doctor's appointment that ran late.

    b. A co-worker kept talking to me.

3. a. The cause was that we don't have flexible work hours.

    b. We have a personality difference. I'm quiet and shy; the co-worker is talkative and outgoing.

Developing Strategies to Resolve Conflicts, pages 44–45

Answers will vary. Sample answer for the first conflict described above:

By thinking that the work policy wasn't fair, I was letting the problem become personal. I focused on our goal—to get the job done. I developed two plans: **(1)** to have flexible hours all the time, and **(2)** to have flexible hours for doctors' appointments and the kids' school activities. I chose the second plan because I thought it was more reasonable from my supervisor's point of view. Then I asked my supervisor if it would be possible for me to work flexible hours for doctors' appointments, etc. That way I could get the work done instead of just losing those hours. My supervisor said we might be able to work it out and for me to talk with her about it the next time I have to take time for an appointment. In the future, I'll try to keep things less personal and remember that when my boss corrects me, she's just trying to do her job.

Developing Strategies for Difficult Situations, page 45

Answers will vary. Sample answer: I felt that this new co-worker was kind of stuck-up because he always refused when we asked him to go out with us after work. One day, I started kidding around and called him a stick-in-the-mud in front of the whole gang. He explained that while he would like to get to know us better, it was against his religion to drink or dance. Later, I apologized and asked if he would like to join us for a cup of coffee sometime. He smiled and said if we didn't mind his drinking herbal tea instead, he'd be happy to go. If I had it to do all over again, I wouldn't have made fun of him in front of everybody else. He's actually a nice guy.

WorkSkills, pages 46–47

Answers will vary. Sample answers:

1. You may be right, but the important thing is to be sure to type the main points of your conversation or the payment terms that the debtor has agreed to. Do you understand how to get into the comment section, Lillian?

2. Actually, we don't keep written records of the debtor's account anymore. Typing your comments into the computer will take a while for you to get used to, but I'm sure you'll do fine.

3. Lillian, the form letters are already set up and will save you a lot of time and aggravation. Besides, I think you'll find it pretty neat the way all the debtor and client information automatically fills in the right places in the letters. I was always afraid I'd type a wrong number or something. Now the computer enters all the information with one push of the F7 key. Just give the form letters a try for a while. If you still don't like it, we can discuss it again.

4. I'm not positive, but I think you're having a hard time accepting that our procedures are different from the ones you're used to. Is that part of the problem, Lillian?

5. Lillian, you have a lot of experience that we need in our company. The collectors have a weekly meeting at which we discuss procedures for handling certain debtor situations. I think you'll have a lot to share with us at these meetings. Will you be willing to offer your advice during these meetings?

Read It, page 47

Tips will vary. If possible, write down and share tips specific to the type of work you do. For example, if you work in an office in which you do clerical work for many different people, try to find tips for setting priorities and explaining them to others.

Review, pages 48–50

STEP 1: Apply Your Skills

1. Answers will vary. Some possible people to speak with at work include a supervisor or co-worker; outside of work you might speak with a salesclerk, your child's teacher, or committee or group members you're associated with.

2. sometime within the next few days

3. Answers will vary. Any purpose should be to inform, explain, or persuade the other person about something.

4. Answers will vary. The outcome should be directly related to the purpose of the conversation.

STEP 2: Self-Evaluation

1. You should have answered *Yes* to items a–l. Make note of any statements you answered *No* to. These indicate the skills you need to improve.

2. Compare the outcome of the conversation to your desired outcome (step 1, question 4). They should be the same.

3. Select only those skills that you applied successfully.

4. Select skills that you answered *No* to.

STEP 3: Personal Action Plan

1. Select two or three skills that you answered *No* to.

2. Select ten days in the near future.

3. Write down skills you answered *No* to; then explain specifically what you will do to apply them in the future.

4. Select a method that appeals to you, so that you will actually use it.

5. Evaluate yourself honestly.

PROGRAM 11: WORKING TOGETHER

Developing Teamwork Skills, page 56

Answers will vary. If you are a member of an effective team, you will have written *True* for all five items. If you wrote *False* for some items, analyze why and think about what you might have done to improve these areas.

Approaching a Task as a Team Player, pages 56–57

1. No
2. No
3. Yes
4. No
5. No

Building a Teamwork Approach, page 57

Answers will vary. Make an honest effort to improve your weaker qualities, and remember that anything you offer to the team will strengthen your teamwork skills as well as the team itself.

WorkSkills, pages 58–59

1. He noticed a problem and asked Joe about it. Waddell discussed with Joe the problem and its causes.

2. Answers will vary. Sample answers: The workers writing the work orders could be trained on how to make the orders clearer. Waddell could send the work orders to the print shop an hour earlier so the press supervisor can review them and call the print shop with questions before everyone goes home for the day. The press room could form a team to evaluate problem orders, develop several choices on how to proceed, and then go with the best choice.

3. Answers will vary. Sample answer: Making a better order form and training the order writers are the best choices because they save time and money and will prevent mistakes. Paying for a messenger service four times a day will be too expensive. Holding jobs until the next day will delay the entire day's press work. The press people still may not want to call Waddell in the middle of the night. Sending the work orders earlier in the day is OK, except any orders received from customers late in the day will already be one day behind schedule. Forming a press team to evaluate confusing orders is good, except the customer still may not like the way the print job came out.

4. They could form a team to develop a new order form. Then they could hold a brief joint meeting between the print shop workers and the press persons to show them the proper way to write and read the orders.

5. If the number of mistakes in customers' print jobs decreases, then the plan has solved the problem. If the mistakes continue, they need to develop a new plan.

Tech Tip, page 59

Both faxing and e-mail would save time. However, if the company entered the form on computer, Waddell could key the order directly into the computer and then e-mail it to the press room.

Participating on a Work Team, page 60

1. Group
2. Team
3. Team
4. Group
5. Team

Participating on an Organized Work Team, pages 60–61

Answers will vary. Sample answers:
Work Team: Develops a plan of action. Assigns tasks to each team member. Puts the plan into effect. Team members share responsibility for the outcome. Team members support each other, whether the plan succeeds or fails.
Sports Team: Develops a game plan. Every team member is responsible for own position. On game day, the team puts the game plan into effect. Team members share responsibility for the outcome of the game. Team members support each other, whether they win or lose.

Sharing Responsibility for the Outcome, page 61

Answers will vary. First, you should have identified the needs of the team. Then the skills, ideas, and resources you listed should have been aimed at meeting those needs.

WorkSkills, pages 62–63

1. At the start, the group is not working as a team, instead blaming others and refusing to take responsibility for finding solutions. By the end of the conversation, it is working together as a team to find a solution.

2. Answers will vary. Sample answer: Jesse and Consuela both show good leadership skills. Jesse, however, took the initiative to speak up first to get the discussion on a positive track. Therefore, he shows the best leadership skills.

3. Answers will vary. Sample answer: No. Everyone has a right to his or her ideas, and Maurice's views can help the team see another dimension of the situation. But the team should learn to handle negative reactions, and Maurice should learn to state his ideas in a more positive way.

4. When Consuela said, "I think we can come up with good ideas," she got everyone on task. Before she spoke up, team members were talking about management, which was not the purpose of the meeting.

5. Yes. After Max suggested that they write the questionnaire, the three other team members gave their approval.

6. Answers will vary. Sample answer: They will probably work well together. There's a good mix of workers who have definite ideas about their work. The group quickly reached a consensus on the first step to be taken.

7. Answers will vary. Sample answer: The team members shouldn't be discouraged or blame each other. Instead, they should ask management to explain why certain ideas were not accepted. That way, the team can build on management's decisions as they revise the current plan or develop a new plan.

Write It, page 63

Answers will vary. Ideas may range from physical changes in the surroundings to training of people so they are aware of various dangers and of how to prevent them.

Being Part of an Effective Team, page 64

1-2. Answers will vary. Once you know which leadership skills and interpersonal and problem-solving skills you need to develop, you can work toward becoming a good leader and team member.

Balancing the Individual with the Whole to Meet Goals, pages 64–65

1. Yes
2. No
3. Yes
4. No
5. Yes
6. Yes

Organizing to Function as a Successful Team, page 65

1-2. Answers will vary. Refer to the leadership skills listed on page 64.

WorkSkills, pages 66–67

1. a, b, d, e, f, g
2. a, b, c, e, f
3. d, e
4. a
5. a, b, c, d, e, f
6. The team kept its goal in mind while considering Imelda's needs. Then Irma and Jay took over some responsibilities that would let Imelda meet her needs as well as enabling the team to meet its goal.
7. Answers will vary. Sample answer: Rating: 4. The team shows a good balance of leadership skills, but some members, like Lucy and Imelda, could develop their leadership skills more. The interpersonal and problem-solving skills also were balanced. Jay and Irma both suggested things they could do to make the change work.

Mayela, however, could have been more supportive in the beginning. Before Imelda asked about working the buttonholer, she could have said that she didn't want to hold back the team from its goal. However, the team did resolve its problem and did it quickly.

Math Matters, page 67

Multiply the bonus per blouse by the number of blouses made in one week. Then divide by the number of team members.
$0.60 \times 325 = 195
$195 \div 5 = 39
Each team member will earn a $39 bonus.

Review, pages 68–70

STEP 1: Apply Your Skills

1. Answers will vary. At work, you might communicate with formal teams that have been organized to work on specific problems or goals. In your personal life, you might work with your children and their teachers to produce desired outcomes, with neighbors to improve conditions in your community, or with a church or other religious group to plan an outing.
2. sometime within the next few days
3. Answers will vary. Some possible purposes include achieving a desired goal, resolving problems, and gathering information and facts.
4. Answers will vary. The outcome should be related to the team's purpose.

STEP 2: Self-Evaluation

1. You should have answered *Yes* to items a–k. Make note of any statements you answered *No* to. These indicate the skills you need to improve.
2. Compare the outcome of the conversation to your desired outcome (step 1, question 4). They should be the same.
3. Select only those skills that you applied successfully.
4. Select skills that you answered *No* to.

STEP 3: Personal Action Plan

1. Select two or three skills that you answered *No* to.
2. Select ten days in the near future.
3. Write down skills you answered *No* to; then explain specifically what you will do to apply them in the future.
4. Select a method that appeals to you so that you will actually use it.
5. Evaluate yourself honestly.

PROGRAM 12: COMMUNICATING WITH CUSTOMERS

Understanding the Importance of Customer Satisfaction, page 76

1. True
2. False
3. True
4. False

Providing Customer Service, pages 76–77

1. Positive
2. Negative
3. Positive
4. Negative
5. Negative

Understanding How Customer Satisfaction Benefits You, page 77

Answers will vary. If you provided good customer service, you probably answered customers' questions, referred customers to the appropriate person or department, listened to customers' complaints, or helped solve customers' problems. When you were able to satisfy the customers, you probably had a good feeling about yourself and your work.

As a customer, you may have benefited from good customer service by having a difficult situation resolved.

WorkSkills, pages 78–79

1. (3)
2. (4)
3. (2)

Read It, page 79

Answers will vary. Explanations should identify the services offered by the business, such as electronic banking and free checking, and tell how these services help meet customers' needs.

Providing for Customers' Needs, page 80

1. U
2. I
3. PS
4. U
5. PS

Identifying Problem Situations, page 81

Answers will vary. Sample answers:
Satisfaction. Tone: pleasant; Face: smiling; Body: relaxed
Frustration. Tone: tense; Face: stern; Body: tense
Patience. Tone: gentle; Face: relaxed; Body: relaxed
Impatience. Tone: harsh; Face: frowning; Body: tense
Anger. Tone: threatening; Face: frowning; Body: tense

Ensuring Customer Satisfaction, page 81

Answers will vary. You should identify what specific actions you needed the employee or company to take to make you a satisfied customer.

WorkSkills, pages 82–83

1. (3)
2. (1)
3. (2)
4. (1)
5. Answers will vary. Sample answer: Call Mrs. Bell, apologize, and ask her what would make her happy. If possible, do what she asks. If not possible, offer an alternative solution.

Math Matters, page 83

$20\% \times \$688.72 = .20 \times \$688.72 = \$137.74$ refund on vinyl floor.
$15\% \times \$1,094.40 = .15 \times \$1,094.40 = \$164.16$ discount on carpeting.
$\$164.16 - 137.74 = \$26.42$
The discount on the carpeting would save her \$26.42 more than the refund on the vinyl flooring.

Working with Difficult Customers, page 84

1. Answers will vary. The customer service representative should have stayed calm and worked to solve the problem that was making you unhappy.
2. Answers will vary. The customer service representative should have stayed calm by approaching the situation as if the situation, not you, were difficult. Then he or she should have asked how you wanted the situation resolved and tried to meet your needs.

Developing Strategies for Dealing with Customer Complaints, pages 84–85

1. b
2. a
3. a
4. b

Using Problem-Solving Language, page 85

Answers will vary. Possible response: I spoke calmly and let the person know I was concerned about the problem. Then I asked what the person thought the cause of the problem was and how the problem should be resolved. Finally, we discussed a mutually agreeable solution.

WorkSkills, pages 86–87

1. He paid in full for new brakes, but the new brakes squeak.

2. He would have to wait again to have the brakes looked at.

3. Gina failed to follow the following *do's*: make repeat business your goal; stay and sound calm; find a solution; refer the customer to someone else when necessary. Gina also should have avoided these *don'ts*: don't take it personally; don't get baited.

4. Answers will vary. Sample answer: "Mr. Turro, we'll be glad to look at the brakes, but you probably don't want to wait until these customers' cars have been serviced. Would it be possible for you to bring your car in on Tuesday or Wednesday morning?"

5. Answers will vary. One possible solution: Make an appointment for Mr. Turro to bring the car in on Tuesday or Wednesday morning as soon as possible so he doesn't have to wait. Alternate solution: Ask Mr. Turro if Gina could drive him home so the mechanic could look at the car after the other customers' cars have been serviced. Then when the brakes are fixed, Gina could drop off the car at Mr. Turro's house.

Write It, page 87

Answers will vary. Sample answer: You should get involved in the conversation between Gina and Mr. Turro as soon as possible. Apologize and assure him that you want the job to be done correctly. Calmly and clearly explain your problem with the customers who are waiting; explain that you want to give them the same courtesies you showed Mr. Turro yesterday when he waited. Suggest a solution. If it's not agreeable, offer an alternate solution. If it's not agreeable, ask Mr. Turro how he would resolve the problem; then try to find a mutually agreeable solution.

Review, pages 88–90

STEP 1: Apply Your Skills

1. Answers will vary.

2. Some possible business conversations with customers might include face-to-face transactions or telephone problem-solving discussions; some possible "personal business" conversations as a customer might include discussions with salesclerks to get information about products you would like to buy or problem-solving discussions with salesclerks and business operators.

3. Answers will vary. The outcome should be related to the purpose of the conversation.

STEP 2: Evaluation

1–9. Answers will vary. You should answer these questions as soon after the conversation as possible.

10. Answers will vary. Compare the actual outcome of the customer communication with what you had hoped would be the outcome. (See your answer to step 1, question 3.)

STEP 3: Personal Action Plan

1. Select two or three skills you marked *No*.

2. Answers will vary. For the skills identified in question 1, you should explain specifically what you will do to apply them in the future.

3. Select a method that appeals to you so that you will actually use it.

4. Evaluate yourself honestly.

PROGRAM 13: A PROCESS FOR WRITING

Becoming an Effective Writer, page 96
1–4. Answers will vary based on personal experience.

Writing Is Critical to Business Success, pages 96–97
a, c, e

Adapting the Writing Process to Fit Your Needs, page 97

1. step 6: Proofread your final draft for errors.

2. step 3: Select an appropriate format.

3. step 4: Write a first draft.

4. step 7: Distribute your writing.

5. step 1: Identify your purpose and audience.

6. step 5: Review and revise your first draft.

7. step 2: Gather facts and organize your thoughts.

WorkSkills, pages 98–99

1. a. find out what work needs to be done
   b. track his work and the amount of time spent per task

2. a. assign tasks
   b. review work that has been done

3. A form. The form labels and organizes the information. This makes it easier to quickly locate necessary information.

4. No, because he forgot to fill in the start and finish dates, and he misspelled words.

5. Rubin should follow step 6 (proofread your final draft) to be sure he lists facts accurately and completely and spells words correctly.

Communicate, page 99

Answers will vary. Sample conversation:

Supervisor: Rubin, you did a good job on the boiler.

Rubin: Thanks, boss.

Supervisor: But, when you fill out a work order report, I really need you to make sure that you fill in all the necessary information. For one thing, our warranties are valid only when we can prove we did proper maintenance. Try to watch your spelling, too, will you, Rubin? And be sure to date your reports.

Rubin: I sure will. Thanks for letting me know. I'll be more careful.

Understanding Workplace Writing, page 100

1. H
2. DNB
3. H
4. H
5. H
6. DNB

Focusing on the Audience, pages 100–101

Answers will vary. Sample answer: The workshop provides information that will help you write better, faster, and with less effort. You will find it worth your time, I'm sure. To register, please sign the sheet on my desk.

Ensuring the Material Is Well Presented, page 101

Answers will vary. You should rewrite the memo so that it is free of errors.

WorkSkills, pages 102–103

See answers below.

TOPNOTCH TA APPLIANCES

Credit Request for Returned Merchandise

Date Received: November 23, 1998   **Purchase Order #:** 84490

Customer Name: Fred Kolac, Holly's Kitchenware House

Address: 10368 Merchant's Lane

City: Columbus   **State:** OH   **ZIP:** 43218

Item	Item #	Price	Quantity	Total Price
Topnotch Super Power Mixers	M-71105	$120.99	10	$1,209.90

COMMENTS   **Date:** November 23, 1998

Reason for Return: 10 Power Mixers were sent to customer instead of 10 Topnotch Blenders.

Action Needed: Credit customer's account $1,209.90 for returned Power Mixers.

Shipping/Receiving Clerk: Corliss

Communicate, page 103

Answers will vary. Sample main points:

1. Calling to apologize
2. Letting you know what we're doing to correct the error
3. Credited your account
4. Shipped the replacement items
5. Let me know if you have any more problems

Using Appropriate Language, page 104

1.	Slang	6.	Formal
2.	Formal	7.	Formal
3.	Jargon	8.	Jargon
4.	Slang	9.	Formal
5.	Formal	10.	Formal

Writing Clearly, pages 104–105

State your purpose: Mr. Kolac clearly states the purpose of the letter and explains what he wants to happen.

Use specific examples: By describing what was ordered and what was received, Mr. Kolac gave specific examples.

Make your case: Mr. Kolac should have expressed his feelings about the incorrect error and the problems it has created for his business.

State your desired response: He clearly explained that he wants the ten blenders he originally ordered and that he wants his account credited for the ten mixers he's returning.

Reread what you've written: He may have reread the letter and removed language that was too strong.

Checking Grammar and Usage, page 105

Answers will vary. Be sure your memo is free of errors.

WorkSkills, pages 106–107

Compare your letter to the sample below:

Dear Mr. Schwartz:

[Purpose of letter] Thank you for giving me the opportunity to bid on the installation of a new intercom entry system at the Courtland Apartments, 400-414 Maple Street, Elmhurst, Illinois. My bid follows.

[Special details] Grand Communications will furnish and install a new intercom entry system. The system will serve 45 apartments with 7 lobby entries and 1 front gate entry. Amplifiers will be installed in the basement under each of the 7 lobby areas. Wiring will be done in a neat manner. Warranty on labor and material is two years.

[Cost of materials and labor] Materials and Labor:

(45)	2805 Intercom panels with surface back boxes	$1,000.00
(7)	3705 Dual lobby intercom control amplifiers	1,680.00
(7)	1088 16VAC transformers	2,100.00
(7)	4400 Lobby panels with frame and metal buttons	700.00
(1)	7743 Gate lobby equipment	2,100.00
	TOTAL	$7,580.00

[Payment requirements] Payment Requirements:
- 1/2 of total required as a down payment.
- Balance due when system is operating correctly.

[Your desired response] Please call me within 30 days if you wish to accept this bid. Thank you for considering Grand Communications for this job.

Very truly yours,

Mark Wilton

Mark Wilton
Sales Representative

Read It, page 107

You should have corrected all spelling, grammar, sentence structure, and punctuation mistakes.

Review, pages 108–110

Review Checklist

1. a. Yes
    b. No
    c. No
    d. No
    e. No
    f. No

Proofreading Checklist

2. a. No
    b. No
    c. No
    d. No
    e. No
    f. No
    g. Yes

Final Draft

3. Answers will vary. Compare your final draft to the sample draft below.

Quality Home Contractors

2681 N. Long Avenue • Chicago, Illinois 60657
773-499-7997 • FAX 773-499-7998

FAX TRANSMITTAL

TO: _Kathie Zeco, Sales Representative_

FROM: _Dittmar Schaefer, Product Representative_

DATE: _October 23, 1998_

SUBJECT: _Defective Siding_

MESSAGE:

Attached is a copy of the letter we received from Profit Products' quality control

coordinator, Joe Mardean. It explains why the siding they supplied us is defective

and what the company has done to correct the problem. I know that your

customers the Newmans are upset, and rightfully so; the letter should help you

explain to them how the problem occurred. When you speak with them,

please ask what day they would like us to come next week to replace the siding.

Then let me know what they say so I can schedule the job. Thank you for your help,

Kathie. Please call if you have any questions.

NO. OF PAGES INCLUDING COVER PAGE: _2_

Dittmar Schaefer

PROGRAM 14: SUPPLYING INFORMATION: DIRECTIONS, FORMS, AND CHARTS

Writing Down Information, page 116

Answers will vary. Sample answers:

shopping list	reminded me what to buy
time sheet	informed me and company how many hours I worked
note to co-worker	reminded me and co-worker of deadline
file folder label	made it easier to find filed papers
calendar notes	helped me schedule appointments

Tracking Information Through Writing, pages 116–117

Answers will vary. Sample answers:

1. to-do list and list of back orders

2. helped me schedule work to be done; helped inform customers placing telephone orders that certain items are on back order

Writing Clear Instructions, page 117

Answers will vary. Sample answer:
How to Sort Incoming Mail

1. Mail is delivered to receptionist around 9:30 each morning.

2. Receptionist divides the mail into piles for each accountant.

3. Mail that is not addressed to a specific accountant is put in the office manager's pile.

4. When every piece of mail has been sorted, the receptionist uses the telephone intercoms to each secretary to let them know the mail is ready.

5. The secretaries will pick up the mail for their bosses.

WorkSkills, pages 118–119

1.

> **Aisle 21**
>
> KITCHEN SINKS
> KITCHEN FAUCETS

2. Answers will vary but should refer to the inventory check and the date. Sample answer:

> **INVENTORY CHECK**
>
> Completed July 11, 1998, by Shanti

3. Shanti put a checkmark by an item number when the quantity in the warehouse matched the quantity listed on the report.

4. the actual quantity in the warehouse if it was different from the quantity on the report

5. KSP-6052, KSS-6060, KSS-6062, KSP-6071, KFS-6070, KFS-6071, KFS-6072

Math Matters, page 119

Total number of items on printout	106
Total number of actual items in warehouse	− 105
Difference	1

If the store's records are inaccurate, they might run out of an item without knowing it or order too many of another item.

Working with Forms, page 120

1. c
2. h
3. d
4. a
5. g
6. e
7. f
8. b

Filling Out Forms, pages 120–121

Answers will vary but should name three forms, each with a purpose, due date (or time), and information needed to complete the form. They should also be neat and accurate. Sample answer:

1. Bank deposit and withdrawal forms. **Purpose**: to add and deduct money from bank accounts; **Due**: as necessary; **Information**: account numbers, amount of deposit or withdrawal, name and address

2. Health insurance claim form. **Purpose**: to submit doctors' bills to insurance company for payment; **Due**: as soon after doctor's visit as possible; **Information**: insurance group number, identification number, member's name, address, Social Security number, date of birth, phone number, and copy of bill from doctor

3. Team member shift report form. **Purpose**: to explain a specific problem with a machine or leave information the next shift needs; **Due**: end of each shift; **Information**: worker's name, date, shift, machine number, hours worked, remarks or comments

Gathering Information from Completed Forms, page 121

Answers will vary. Sample answers: customer or vendor purchase order forms, accident report forms, tax forms, insurance forms, job evaluation forms

WorkSkills, pages 122–123

See answers below.

HEALTH·RITE
EXERCISE EQUIPMENT
2108 Wilshire Boulevard • Reno, NV 89557

DATE: 12/05/99
BILL TO:
Philip Friker

Otus Office Center

3421 Market Street, Suite 2000

San Francisco, CA 94114

INVOICE NO. P47731
SHIPPED TO:
Philip Friker

Otus Office Center

3421 Market Street, Suite 2000

San Francisco, CA 94114

ITEM # DESCRIPTION	QUANTITY ORDERED	QUANTITY SHIPPED	UNIT PRICE	AMOUNT
3057HPT High Perf. Treadmill	2	2	$649.99	$1,299.98
27549ATS Arctic Track Ski Machine	2	2	349.99	699.98
234HPS High Perform. Stepper	2	2	289.99	579.98

SUBTOTAL	2,579.94
SHIPPING & HANDLING	108.79
TOTAL	$2,688.73

Using Charts Effectively, page 124

Answers will vary. Sample answers:
1. postal rate chart
2. to calculate the amount of postage needed to ship packages
3. a calendar to schedule my time and appointments

Learning How Charts Are Organized, pages 124–125

1. (1)
2. (4)
3. (4)

Completing Charts, page 125

1. list the schedule of employees' workdays and hours

2. names of employees, number of workers needed at each time slot each day, days and times when more workers are needed, availability of each employee

3. 12/7

WorkSkills, pages 126–127

1. juice oranges, ruby red grapefruit

2. new tangelos, honeybell tangelos, temple oranges, honey tangerines

3. February

4. June

5. The chart. It organizes the information in a way that is easier to read and understand.

FRUIT SEASONS	Nov.	Dec.	Jan.	Feb.	Mar.	Apr.	May	Jun.
New tangelos	X	X						
Navel oranges	X	X	X	X	X			
Juice oranges	X	X	X	X	X	X	X	X
Honeybell tangelos			X	X				
Temple oranges		X	X	X	X			
Honey tangerines					X	X		
Valencia oranges						X	X	X
Ruby red grapefruit	X	X	X	X	X	X	X	
Pink grapefruit	X	X	X	X	X	X	X	
White grapefruit	X	X	X	X	X	X	X	

Tech Tip, page 127

See answers below.

1. No
2. No
3. No
4. No
5. The form should be completed as follows:

PLEASANT CONVALESCENT CENTER

PATIENT'S PROPERTY INVENTORY FORM. COMPLETE THIS FORM FOR EVERY PATIENT ADMITTED TO THE CENTER.

Patient's name: _Jerzy Kowalski_
Address: _817 Collman Avenue_
City: _Grass Valley_   State: _CA_   Zip: _95945_
Telephone: _916-555-8118_

IN CASE OF AN EMERGENCY, CONTACT:

Name: _Katarzyna Kowalski_
Telephone: _916-555-2222_
Relation to patient: _Daughter_

THE PATIENT HAS BEEN ADMITTED WITH THE FOLLOWING PERSONAL PROPERTY:

Jewelry: _1 gold wristwatch_
1 gold wedding band

Electronics: _1 electric razor_

Clothing: _2 prs. shoes: gym; slippers_   _2 warm-up suits_
5 prs. underwear

Miscellaneous: _1 deck playing cards_   _1 denture cleaner_
4 hardcover books   _1 wallet with ID only_
1 pr. eyeglasses   _1 deodorant_
1 upper denture

Patient's signature: _Jerzy Kowalski_   Administrator's initials: _aL_

PROGRAM 15: WRITING MEMOS AND LETTERS

Planning Written Communication, page 136

Answers will vary but should include four items and a purpose for each. Sample answers:

1. **Item:** report from bank; **Purpose:** to inform me of account activity

2. **Item:** letter from customer; **Purpose:** to explain why the bill will not be paid in full

3. **Item:** memo from my boss; **Purpose:** to inform me of a report she needs

4. **Item:** note to supervisor; **Purpose:** to request vacation time

Step 1: Identifying Your Purpose and Audience, page 136

Answers will vary. Sample answers:

1. a company's human resources manager

2. No relationship. Because I don't know this person, I will identify myself and use formal language.

Step 2: Gathering Facts and Organizing Your Thoughts, page 137

1. When?
2. Who?
3. What?
4. How?
5. Where?
6. Why?

WorkSkills, pages 138–139

1. The form should contain the information shown below.

2. to make sure he had understood correctly

IMPORTANT MESSAGE

FOR   _Ms. Jackson_

DATE   _[today's date]_

M   _s. Lucita Grey_

OF   _customer_

PHONE NUMBER   _(work) 555-991-3377_

- ☐ Telephoned you
- ☐ Visited you
- ☐ Returned your call
- ☑ Please return call
- ☐ Caller will call again
- ☐ URGENT

MESSAGE : _Ms. Grey was in our store and clerk ordered a men's brown leather jacket with front zipper—merchandise number 4591459, style number 31751, sale price $200—from Lakeside, MI store. They were to send it right away. Customer hasn't received it yet. Jacket is birthday gift for husband. Wants coat sent to daughter's house at 6333 Arnold, Westmont, IL 60126. It was paid with a credit card. Please call asap._

SIGNED   _Pete_

Math Matters, page 139

$300 – $200 = $100
$100 ÷ $300 = 0.3333
The percent markdown was about 33%.

Step 3: Selecting a Format, page 140

Answers will vary. Sample answer: I received a memo from my supervisor. The purpose was to inform me of a training session on some new equipment we will receive next week. My supervisor used the memo format for this message because it was an "inside" business message.

Looking at Memos, Letters, and Reports, pages 140–141

1. Memo
2. Report
3. Letter

Step 4: Writing a First Draft, page 141

1. G
2. B
3. B
4. G

WorkSkills, pages 142–143

1. to inform the distributor of damaged figurines
2. business letter
3. bad news format
4. The draft should be organized in the format shown at the bottom of this page.

Communicate, page 143

Answers will vary. Sample answer:

- apologize
- will take action to prevent breakage from happening again
- appreciate the business from A Piece of Europe

Writing and Distributing Final Drafts, page 144

Reviewing and revising first drafts ensure that they are clear and easy to understand. You also want to appear competent.

Step 5: Reviewing and Revising First Drafts, page 144

You should have answered *No* to the last two questions.

- The language should be more formal. "Thanks a bunch . . ." is not appropriate.
- The tone should be more businesslike when the language is corrected. The sentence that begins "Too bad that when I . . ." sounds sarcastic and should be changed.

Step 6: Proofreading the Final Draft, page 144

See the final draft below.

File   Edit   View   Insert   Format   Font   Tools   Window   Help

Untitled1

A Piece of Europe
1337 W. 55th Street
Stahlstown, PA 15687

[today's date]

Ms. Angela Wright
Imports Inc.
9645 S. Lincoln Avenue
Baltimore, MD 21218

Dear Ms. Wright:

This morning, we **received** the ten porcelain figurines that we ordered on the first of the month (Catalog No. 91875). **Thank you** for the prompt shipment.

Unfortunately, when I unpacked the figurines, I discovered that six of them were **damaged.** The figurines are popular with our customers, so we would like them **replaced.** Please issue a return authorization number, arrange for pickup of the damaged goods, and send us six replacements as soon as possible. Because the holiday shopping season is almost here, we need the replacements by the end of the month.

We appreciate your prompt attention to this matter.

Sincerely,

Tomas Barca

Page 1   Normal

Step 7: Distributing Your Writing, page 145

1. Fax, e-mail, or a messenger service would deliver the letter to the recipient in minutes or hours.

2. Mail would be appropriate.

3. Putting the memo in each person's mailbox, sending it by e-mail, or posting it on a company bulletin board would notify all employees.

4. It's a routine report being sent to co-workers, so putting the report in each person's mailbox would be appropriate.

WorkSkills, pages 146–147

1. to prevent playground injuries

2. teachers

3. *Who?* Bobby Feeny; Gilda Stein

   What? cut his knee; broke her arm

   When? Monday, April 10; Wednesday, April 12

   Where? on the playground

   Why? were playing too rough

   How? watch children more carefully

4. a memo, because she's sending it to her co-workers

5. Wording may vary, but the facts and format should match the sample to the right.

6. You should have made the following corrections in paragraph 1: Some of the injuries were really bad (or serious). . . . Bobby Feeny had to get stitches in his knee.

7. a. photocopy it and put it in each teacher's mailbox

   b. post it in the teachers' lounge

MEMO

To: All Teachers
From: Tanya Brobat
Subject: Playground Injuries
Date: Friday, April 14

We seem to have a problem on our hands. Lately, more kids than usual have been getting hurt during recess. Some of the injuries were really bad. On Monday, April 10, Bobby Feeny had to get stiches in his knee. On Wednesday, April 12, Gilda Stein broke her arm.

None of us wants to see our children hurt during playtime. Let's do what we can to watch for behavior that may cause injuries. Thanks for your cooperation!

Communicate, page 147

Answers will vary. Sample answer:

Tanya: I'm sorry to hear you feel that way, Alberto. I've seen you out on the playground, and I know you supervise the children very carefully. I didn't mean to accuse any of the teachers of being careless. I just wanted to inform them of what's been happening and ask them to help prevent further injuries. I'm sure that's a goal we all share.

Review, pages 148–150

Planning Written Communications

1. Ms. Fodor

2. businesslike, neatly handwritten, and free of errors

3. to inform and persuade in order to get a job

4. a. your name

   b. general office assistant

   c. You should have listed skills that match or exceed those requested in the ad.

   d. your address

   e. times you can be reached

   f. You should have listed reasons you would like the job.

   g. your phone number

Organizing and Writing First Drafts

1. handwritten business letter

2. The ad requested this format.

3. good news

4. because the news is neutral or good, rather than bad

5. Answers will vary but should use the format of the sample letter shown next.

Writing and Distributing Final Drafts

1. **Review Checklist:** You should be able to answer *Yes* to questions a–g.

2. Answers will vary but should use the format of the sample letter below.

3. You should be able to say *Yes* to all the questions.

4. Distribute the letter by mailing it. This is the best option, because a fax of a handwritten letter would not be clear or professional looking, and a messenger would be expensive.

Your Name
Your Address

Ms. Fodor, Human Resources
Tower & King
c/o The Times
P.O. Box 620
Lexington, KY 40502

Today's Date

Dear Ms. Fodor:

I saw your ad in Sunday's <u>Times</u> for a general office assistant, and I would like to apply for the job. Please consider my qualifications for the position.

As a graduate of the business program at Majors High School, I would bring to the job a strong knowledge of general office procedures. At Majors, I also was trained in basic telephone etiquette and in working with office machines, including photocopiers, faxes, and electronic mail systems. Perhaps most important, I am eager to work and learn more about office procedures firsthand. You can count on me to learn quickly and to do whatever needs to be done.

To arrange for an interview, please call me during business hours at 555-0472. I look forward to speaking with you and learning more about Tower & King.

Sincerely,
Your Name

Glossary

active listening strategies: steps for concentrating on and understanding messages

alternative: a choice from among two or more things

audience: recipients; readers; people who are to receive a message

body language: gestures and postures that communicate messages

business letters: formal written messages sent to customers or business associates

charts: sheets of information arranged in columns and rows

checklists: series of tasks or steps that can be checked off as they are done

columns: information arranged in lines going down a chart

committees: groups, often temporary, that are formed to solve a specific problem or meet a specific goal

communication: the process of sending and receiving messages

competition: businesses that offer similar products or services to a similar customer base

complimentary closing: a formal ending to a business letter, such as *Yours truly*

conflict resolution: the settling of disagreements by finding common goals

conflicts: disagreements between people who have different goals

customer base: a business's current and potential customers

customer satisfaction: the degree to which customers' expectations are met

customer service: help a business offers its clients to make a good impression about its products or services

customer service representatives: employees who specialize in taking customers' orders, providing product or service information, and handling customer complaints

distribute: to send or deliver a written message to intended receivers

diversity: variety; differences

draft: a version of a written message

e-mail: messages that are keyed into a computer and sent electronically

ethnic: relating to a large group of people classed according to common racial, national, religious, or cultural backgrounds or origins

faxes: written messages that are copied on a fax machine and sent using telephone signals

feedback: an evaluation of an action or process, such as feedback a supervisor gives to employees about their work

"five *Ws* and an *H*": (page 137) fact-gathering questions (*Who? What? Where? When? Why? How?*)

formal language: words and phrases used in formal situations, such as business transactions

format: the form in which a message is organized, written, and set up on one or more pages

forms: typed or printed documents with blank lines and spaces for insertion of requested information

goals: objectives or desired outcomes

graphics: graphs, charts, tables, and other visual representations of data

headings: labels written or printed at the top of columns or before rows to identify information

initiative: self-motivation; effort to solve a work problem or improve work methods

instructions: steps or orders to be completed

interpersonal: between persons, as in interpersonal communication skills

inventory: a complete and detailed list of items, often with their estimated value

invoices: lists of goods sent to a buyer showing the terms of a purchase (prices, amounts, shipping charges, etc.)

jargon: business or technical language that is difficult for people unfamiliar with a business to understand

labels: slips of paper written on and attached to anything for identification or description

leadership: guiding and directing others

lists: series of items, names, words, or phrases

memos: brief written business messages that begin with the standard headings *To, From, Subject, Date*

miscommunications: misunderstandings caused by poor communications

motivate: to provide with an incentive or other reason to take action

nonverbal communication: body language, facial expressions, and voice qualities

order forms: written requests for goods that someone wants to buy or receive

organizational patterns: standard ways to organize a business message

orientation: the process of acquainting oneself with a business, product, or job

perceives: sees and interprets

prejudices: opinions formed without knowing a person or situation firsthand

priorities: tasks that are the most important or that must be done first

procedures: guidelines or rules for doing a job

proofread: to read a message carefully to find and correct errors

purpose: a reason for writing (to inform, to explain, to persuade)

recipient: receiver of a written or spoken message

repeat customers: customers who go to the same business again and again

revise: to rewrite a message to improve it

routine reports: reports that are completed on a regular basis

rows: information arranged in lines going across a chart

salutation: a spoken or written greeting

service standards: written or spoken "rules" that explain customer service goals and the employee's role in meeting them

signs: boards that have been written on for advertising or informative purposes

slang: very informal words and expressions used in informal situations among friends

solicitation: the process of asking for something, such as information

special reports: reports on special subjects

strategies: effective ways of getting something done

subcontractor: an independent worker or business hired by another business to do a specific job

swipe card: a card, similar to a credit card, that has a magnetic strip containing information about the user

to-do lists: lists of a series of tasks that need to be done

touch screen: a computer screen on which a person communicates by touching various options

"you" attitude: an approach to writing in which the reader is given the benefits of taking an action

Index

Problem-Solving Checklists

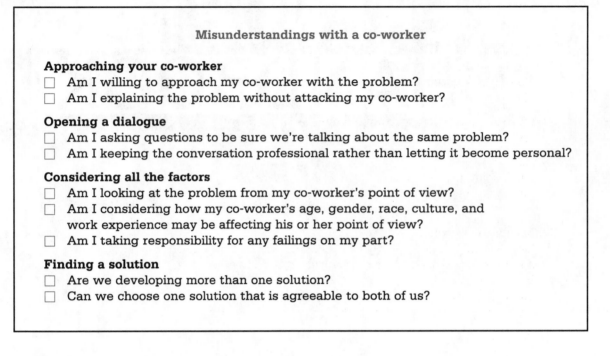

Misunderstandings with a co-worker

Approaching your co-worker
- [ ] Am I willing to approach my co-worker with the problem?
- [ ] Am I explaining the problem without attacking my co-worker?

Opening a dialogue
- [ ] Am I asking questions to be sure we're talking about the same problem?
- [ ] Am I keeping the conversation professional rather than letting it become personal?

Considering all the factors
- [ ] Am I looking at the problem from my co-worker's point of view?
- [ ] Am I considering how my co-worker's age, gender, race, culture, and work experience may be affecting his or her point of view?
- [ ] Am I taking responsibility for any failings on my part?

Finding a solution
- [ ] Are we developing more than one solution?
- [ ] Can we choose one solution that is agreeable to both of us?

Problem solving with a team

Identifying the problem
- [ ] Have we identified the problem that the team needs to resolve?

Generating ideas
- [ ] Am I being cooperative and helpful to other team members?
- [ ] Am I being receptive to other team members' ideas?

Strengthening the team
- [ ] Do my words and actions encourage and motivate my team members?
- [ ] Am I working with team members to explore various solutions?
- [ ] Am I contributing ideas and strategies that strengthen the team?

Misunderstandings with a customer or a client

Taking responsibility
- ☐ Have I apologized to the customer for the problem?
- ☐ Have I admitted any mistakes I or a co-worker have made?

Reaffirming the customer's importance
- ☐ Have I told the customer that his or her business is important to the organization?

Staying focused
- ☐ Am I being positive in my comments and attitude?
- ☐ Am I ignoring any negative comments made by the customer?
- ☐ Am I staying and sounding calm even if the customer is not?

Resolving the problem
- ☐ Have I asked the customer how he or she wants the problem resolved?
- ☐ Am I offering only what my organization can provide?
- ☐ If I am unable to resolve the problem myself, am I referring the customer to someone who can help?
- ☐ Have we chosen a solution that is agreeable to both of us?

Ensuring future customer satisfaction
- ☐ Am I taking steps to ensure the problem won't happen again?

Listening and Speaking Checklists

Active Listening Checklist

Getting ready to listen
- ☐ Have I made eye contact with the speaker?
- ☐ Does my body language say, "I'm ready to listen"?

Focusing on the message
- ☐ Am I ignoring noises and other distractions?
- ☐ Am I concentrating on what the speaker is saying?

Listening for the purpose
- ☐ Have I heard the speaker's main point?
- ☐ What ideas has the speaker given to support the main idea?
- ☐ What do I already know about the topic?

Observing body language
- ☐ What are the speaker's facial expressions, gestures, and body language telling me?
- ☐ Does the speaker's body language match the verbal message?

Asking questions
- ☐ Have I asked questions to check my understanding?

Taking notes
- ☐ Did I write down important facts, instructions, and steps?

Restating what you heard
- ☐ Have I restated the speaker's ideas in my own words?

Effective Speaking Checklist

Knowing your topic
- ☐ What do I want the listener to know?
- ☐ What main points must I tell?
- ☐ In what order will I explain the main points and details?
- ☐ Do I know enough to answer the listener's questions?

Adjusting to the listener's needs
- ☐ Am I thinking about what the listener already knows?
- ☐ Am I explaining any technical terms that the listener doesn't understand?
- ☐ Is the listener's body language telling me that he or she understands?
- ☐ Am I explaining things in another way when the listener looks confused?

Speaking effectively
- ☐ Am I speaking in a natural tone of voice?
- ☐ Do I sound enthusiastic?
- ☐ Am I making eye contact?
- ☐ Am I sticking to the main points and details?
- ☐ Am I repeating important points for emphasis?

Encouraging responses
- ☐ Am I encouraging the listener to ask questions?
- ☐ Have I given the listener time to comment?

Steps in the Writing Process

1. **Identify your purpose and audience.**

   Why are you writing? Is your purpose to inform, to explain, to persuade, or a combination of all three? What do you want your reader to do, think, and feel? Put yourself in your reader's shoes. How much does the reader already know about the subject? What other facts will he or she need? Only write what the reader needs to know.

2. **Gather facts and organize your thoughts.**

   Think about what your audience needs to know. Brainstorm a list of facts by answering the "Five *W*s and an *H*": *Who? What? Where? When? Why? How?*

3. **Select a format in which to write your message.**

   Writing a list or a note may be "good enough" for short writing tasks. But for longer or more formal pieces of writing, write a memo, a business letter, or a report. Choose the format that is most appropriate for your purpose and audience.

4. **Write a first draft.**

   Choose a logical pattern of organization. Follow the "good news" pattern if the message is neutral or positive. Use the "bad news" pattern if your message is negative or upsetting. Then get your thoughts down. Don't worry about grammar, spelling, or punctuation at this point.

   Good News Pattern
   1. State your purpose.
   2. Present necessary facts and details.
   3. Explain actions the reader should take and/or express thanks.

   Bad News Pattern
   1. State neutral news.
   2. State the bad news, giving reasons for the negative situation.
   3. State the action to be taken, if any, and end on a positive note.

5. **Review and revise your first draft.**

   Reread what you've written. Look for parts that don't make sense. Be sure you included the key facts and ideas you gathered earlier. Rewrite the first draft, making all of the changes you wrote on the draft.

6. **Proofread your final draft.**

   Proofread your revised draft. Check for errors in grammar, sentence structure, punctuation, spelling, and capitalization. Rewrite the revised draft as many times as needed to be sure it expresses your thoughts clearly and accurately.

7. **Distribute your writing.**

   Give your final draft to your audience. You can distribute it outside the office by mail, fax, e-mail, or messenger service. Within the office, put it in office Inboxes, on desks, or on bulletin boards.

Correct Sentence Structure

1. **Write in complete sentences.**

   A *complete sentence* contains a subject (who or what the sentence is about) and a verb (what the subject does or is) and expresses a complete thought.

   S   V
   <u>I reviewed</u> the safety team's recommendations.

2. **Look for and correct sentence fragments.**

   A *sentence fragment* is a sentence that is incomplete because (1) it is missing a subject or verb or (2) consists only of a *dependent clause*—a group of words that contains a subject and verb but begins with a *subordinating conjunction*—a joining word like *although*—which makes the thought incomplete. Following are ways to correct a fragment.

   Fragment: The ideas were good. <u>Particularly those for the factory.</u>
   Correction: The ideas were good, particularly those for the factory.

   Fragment: <u>If it rains.</u> We will reschedule the company picnic.
   Correction: If it rains, we will reschedule the company picnic.

3. **Look for and revise run-on sentences.**

   A *run-on* is two complete sentences run together.

   Run-on: John was ill we hired a temp to take his place.

   To correct a run-on, separate the two sentences with a period.

   Correction: John was ill. We hired a temp to take his place.

   Or create a *compound sentence*—two complete sentences joined with a *coordinating conjunction* (and, but, nor, or) or a *conjunctive adverb* (therefore, however, nevertheless, then).

   Correction: John was ill<u>, so</u> we hired a temp to take his place.
   Correction: John was ill<u>; therefore,</u> we hired a temp to take his place.

   Or create a *complex sentence*—an *independent clause*, or complete thought, connected to a *dependent clause*.

   Correction: <u>Because John was ill,</u> we hired a temp to take his place.

Grammar Checklist

☐ **Does each verb agree with its subject?**

Present tense verbs, which express actions that occur daily, must end in -*s* when used with the subjects *he, she, it* or their equivalent.

Examples: <u>She</u> <u>works</u> very quickly. / <u>Marita</u> <u>works</u> very quickly.
Examples: <u>He</u> <u>does</u> the shipping. / <u>Ivan</u> <u>does</u> the shipping.

☐ **Is the irregular verb *to be* formed correctly in the present tense?**

To Be: <u>I</u> <u>am</u> a clerk. <u>Vince</u> <u>is</u> a mechanic. <u>We</u> <u>are</u> happy. <u>Are</u> <u>you</u>?

☐ **Is the past tense formed correctly?**

The past tense expresses actions that already occurred. To form the past of a regular verb, add an -*ed* ending. Irregular verbs change form in the past tense. (If you are not sure of the forms of an irregular verb, check a dictionary.)

Regular Verbs: Bill <u>called</u> yesterday. I <u>talked</u> with him.
Irregular Verbs: He <u>went</u> home, so she <u>ran</u> the store.
To Be: <u>You</u> <u>were</u> right: <u>I</u> <u>was</u> calm, but <u>he</u> <u>was</u> upset. <u>It</u> <u>was</u> unfortunate.

☐ **Is the present perfect tense formed correctly?**

The present perfect tense expresses actions that occurred in the recent past. The present perfect follows this pattern: *has* or *have* + (regular verb with -*ed* ending) or (irregular verb in proper form).

Regular Verbs: <u>I</u> <u>have</u> <u>copied</u> the reports, and <u>he</u> <u>has</u> <u>distributed</u> them.
Irregular Verbs: <u>Elsa</u> <u>has</u> <u>written</u> a reply, and <u>we</u> <u>have</u> <u>sent</u> it.
To Be: <u>He</u> <u>has</u> <u>been</u> late recently; <u>we</u> <u>have</u> <u>been</u> on time.

☐ **Is the past perfect tense formed correctly?**

The past perfect tense expresses the first of two actions that occurred in the past. The past perfect follows this pattern: *had* + (regular verb with -*ed* ending) or (irregular verb in proper form).

Regular Verbs: I <u>had</u> <u>fixed</u> the problem by the time they <u>arrived</u>.
Irregular Verbs: He already <u>had</u> <u>left</u> for lunch when the alarm <u>rang</u>.

☐ **Do all pronouns agree with their *antecedents*—the nouns or pronouns they refer to?**

Example: The <u>company</u> has finished <u>its</u> annual report.
Example: <u>Everyone</u> has <u>his</u> or <u>her</u> faults; nobody is perfect.

Punctuation Checklist

☐ **Does each sentence end with a period, exclamation point, or question mark?**

I am impressed by the thoroughness of the report.
Good work!
Can we create additional teams to help resolve other issues?

☐ **Are items in a series separated with commas?**

We need teams for production, quality control, and shipping.

☐ **Does a comma come before the connecting word in compound sentences?**

I suggested Raphael join a team, and he was open to the idea.

☐ **Does a comma follow the dependent clause at the beginning of a complex sentence?**

If you would convince him of the team's merits, I would be thankful.

☐ **Are introductory words and phrases followed by commas?**

Yes, I can see the benefits of teamwork on the job.
By the way, I haven't seen your name on any of the teams.

☐ **Are commas used to separate items in dates and addresses?**

Please inform the sales reps that we will meet on Wednesday, January 13, 1999, at the Write Inn, 308 Grove Ave., Oak Lawn, Illinois.

☐ **Is the closing of a letter followed by a comma?**

Sincerely,
Very truly yours,

☐ **Are words that introduce a list followed by a colon?**

Bring the following items: a notebook and a pen.

☐ **Does a colon follow the salutation of a business letter?**

Dear Ms. Wallek:
Dear Sir or Madam:

☐ **Are apostrophes used to form the possessives of nouns?**

Carlos's desk
workers' benefits

Sample Memo, Fax, and E-Mail

Memos, faxes, and e-mails have two main parts: a heading and a message.

SAMPLE MEMO

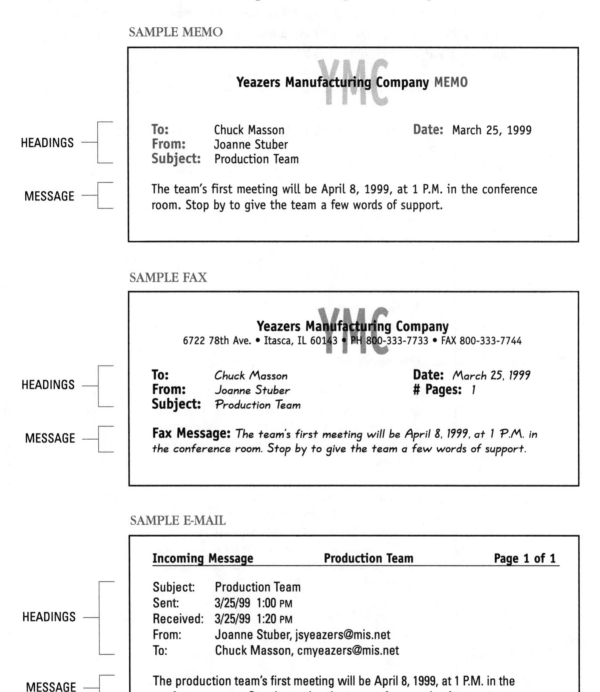

Yeazers Manufacturing Company MEMO

HEADINGS

To: Chuck Masson   **Date:** March 25, 1999
From: Joanne Stuber
Subject: Production Team

MESSAGE

The team's first meeting will be April 8, 1999, at 1 P.M. in the conference room. Stop by to give the team a few words of support.

SAMPLE FAX

Yeazers Manufacturing Company
6722 78th Ave. • Itasca, IL 60143 • PH 800-333-7733 • FAX 800-333-7744

HEADINGS

To: Chuck Masson   **Date:** March 25, 1999
From: Joanne Stuber   **# Pages:** 1
Subject: Production Team

MESSAGE

Fax Message: The team's first meeting will be April 8, 1999, at 1 P.M. in the conference room. Stop by to give the team a few words of support.

SAMPLE E-MAIL

Incoming Message   **Production Team**   **Page 1 of 1**

HEADINGS

Subject: Production Team
Sent: 3/25/99 1:00 PM
Received: 3/25/99 1:20 PM
From: Joanne Stuber, jsyeazers@mis.net
To: Chuck Masson, cmyeazers@mis.net

MESSAGE

The production team's first meeting will be April 8, 1999, at 1 P.M. in the conference room. Stop by to give the team a few words of support.

Sample Business Letter

Business letters have six main parts: the heading, inside address, salutation, body, complimentary closing, and signature. The sample letter below was written on letterhead stationery. If you write a business letter without a letterhead, enter the complete heading: business name, street address, city, state, and ZIP.

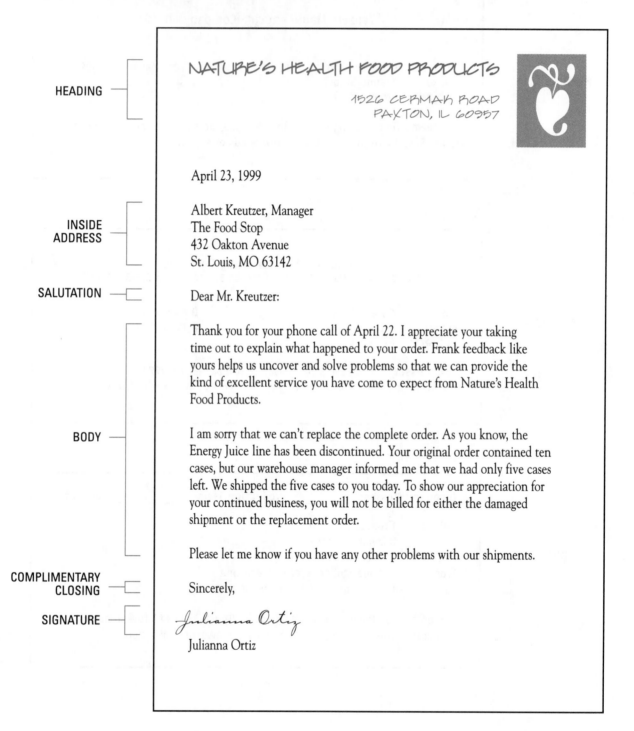

HEADING

NATURE'S HEALTH FOOD PRODUCTS
1526 CERMAK ROAD
PAXTON, IL 60957

April 23, 1999

INSIDE ADDRESS

Albert Kreutzer, Manager
The Food Stop
432 Oakton Avenue
St. Louis, MO 63142

SALUTATION

Dear Mr. Kreutzer:

BODY

Thank you for your phone call of April 22. I appreciate your taking time out to explain what happened to your order. Frank feedback like yours helps us uncover and solve problems so that we can provide the kind of excellent service you have come to expect from Nature's Health Food Products.

I am sorry that we can't replace the complete order. As you know, the Energy Juice line has been discontinued. Your original order contained ten cases, but our warehouse manager informed me that we had only five cases left. We shipped the five cases to you today. To show our appreciation for your continued business, you will not be billed for either the damaged shipment or the replacement order.

Please let me know if you have any other problems with our shipments.

COMPLIMENTARY CLOSING

Sincerely,

SIGNATURE

Julianna Ortiz
Julianna Ortiz